AT EASE IN A BRIGHT RED TIE

IBRAR

John Whiting

AT EASE IN A BRIGHT RED TIE
WRITINGS ON THEATRE

Edited by
Ronald Hayman

OBERON BOOKS
LONDON

First published in 1999 by Oberon Books Ltd.
(incorporating Absolute Classics)
521 Caledonian Road, London N7 9RH
Tel: 0171 607 3637 / Fax: 0171 607 3629
e-mail: oberon.books@btinternet.com

British Library Cataloguing-in-Publication Data
A catalogue record for this book is available from the British Library.

ISBN 1 84002 052 0

Cover photograph: Houston Rogers

Cover design: Andrzej Klimowski

Typography: Richard Doust

Printed in Great Britain by MPG Ltd., Bodmin.

Contents

INTRODUCTION

This book contains a lecture, two interviews, eight statements about the theatre written journalistically or excerpted from notebooks, and twelve critical pieces, all from the most excitingly eventful decade in twentieth-century British theatre history – 1952-62. In the late summer of 1955, London audiences were astonished to find that two tramps were the central characters in a new play called *Waiting for Godot*. In April 1956 a new company opened at the Royal Court Theatre, and four months later the Berliner Ensemble brought three of its productions to the West End. The combination of these three events revolutionised the English theatre. The audience remained predominantly middle-class, but on the stage, working-class accents were no longer heard only from cheeky maids and comic chauffeurs. The catchphrases 'kitchen sink' and 'angry young man' pointed to a radical change of subject-matter. The young man spoke with a gritty provincial accent, and he was angry about everything – especially being underprivileged.

At the same time, the old system of financing productions was being overturned. State subsidy had been almost negligible in the London theatre, except at the Old Vic. During the first six years of its life, the Royal Court never received more than £8000 from the Arts Council, and sometimes only £5000. In the West End, commercial managements were still using money from 'angels' – as the private backers were called – to put on not only drawing-room comedies, thrillers and commercial dramas but also plays by Shakespeare, Congreve, Sheridan and other 'classical' writers, and by new writers such as Harold Pinter and Joe Orton. During the war, the leading management, HM Tennent, which later presented three of John Whiting's plays, had formed a subsidiary company – Tennent Productions Ltd – to stage plays that could be called 'partly educational'. As a non-profit-distributing company, it could claim partial exemption from taxation, and subsidy from the forerunner of the Arts Council – the Council for Entertainment, Music and the Arts (CEMA). But as subsidies became larger, the West End managers, unable to compete with the two new subsidised companies – the National and the Royal Shakespeare – became less active and more commercial.

In 1960 Peter Hall was put in charge of the Shakespeare Memorial Theatre in Stratford-on-Avon. The company had no London base till the end of the year, and did not become the Royal Shakespeare till 1961. Though the National Theatre did not yet exist, many of its actors, directors, designers and administrators started working together in 1962, after Laurence Olivier was appointed as artistic director of the Chichester Festival Theatre – the first large theatre to be built in England with a thrust stage. Of its three first productions, one, *Uncle Vanya,* moved into the National's opening season at the Old Vic.

It is fortunate that John Whiting was writing about theatre at this time of radical change. Few twentieth-century playwrights have written so much criticism. Trained as an actor, blessed with a brain, and blooded as a professional on the stage, he could see the theatre from inside and outside, with love and hatred, realism and idealism, passion and objectivity, sadness and humour. After he died at the age of forty-five in 1963, Peggy Ashcroft said: 'we have lost one of our finest dramatists but also a major critic. Perhaps a critic is even more rare than a dramatist.' She went on to praise his 'marvelously balanced attitude to the theatre – no involvement in one camp or the other but a completely clear and absolutely honest view of his own.'

He was at his best when writing dialogue. Some of his statements about theatre are made in dialogue form, and in many of the other pieces he is carrying on a conversation with himself – interrupting himself with a question or contradiction, and letting his viewpoint shift, if it wants to. It is not only the same velvet voice we find in the criticism as in the plays, but the same sense of humour, the same gift for the poetic turn of phrase, the same eye for significant detail, and the same comic precision in characterising Englishness. And when he writes in the first person, we find something which is not apparent in the plays – a self-mockery or *Selbst-Ironie* that was not always gentle. Like his creative writing, his critical prose is playful, challenging, sophisticated and uncompromisingly intelligent. His work can appeal only to those who like intelligence to be playful and playfulness to be intelligent.

His commentary is relevant to the cultural muddles of today. The crisis in the arts was already being exacerbated by well-meaning critics who felt they should show solidarity with the working class by condemning art that appealed only to an educated minority. Though some plays, obviously, can reach a wider audience than others, the writer cannot address himself to millions of people. For one million to see a production in a theatre with a thousand seats, it would take two and a half years, assuming eight performances were given weekly, and none of the seats was ever empty.

Music-hall used to provide a meeting point between theatre and popular culture, but their only remaining rendezvous is in the musical. Musicals can reach a huge audience by running for ten or more years in a big theatre. This damages non-musical drama by reducing the number of spaces for it.

It was obvious in the Fifties that the only danger to the film and television industries was that standards could sink still lower. It was not obvious that drama and literature could survive without undergoing a radical transformation. In Shakespeare's England, the general may have had no appetite for caviare, but a playwright could run his own company of actors on a low budget. In the Nineteen-Fifties, poets, novelists and painters could go on practising their art so long as they could afford food and lodging, but fringe theatre companies were running into difficulties with the actors' union, Equity, which was imposing minimum levels of salary, while all creative artists were surrounded by a combination of unfriendly pressures – political, social, economic and cultural. In his 1957 lecture at the Old Vic, Whiting complained that:

> what we knew as art is almost imperceptibly being replaced by something else... So many people have to be reached now, all at the same level of comprehension and all at the same time. This has led to a degeneration. I suggest that the voice you hear today in all branches of literature including the theatre is not the individual voice but the collective voice... The writer has become the spokesman not for himself but for a group, an organisation, a class or a sect... The cult of the individual is now almost as great a social crime in the West as it is a political crime in the East.

In the East, Bertolt Brecht was the most influential of the writers who wanted to move art away from the individual. In his plays, the focus was on the group, and he contended that drama should be useful. Its function was to push the audience in the direction of socialism. When I met him shortly before he died in 1956, he was arguing that it was impossible to write a good play in a capitalist country. When I asked what he thought of Sartre's play *Les Mains Sales,* his answer was that he would have to read it again before he could judge. 'You see, I haven't read it since Khruschev's last speech.'* That was the one at the twentieth party congress, when he denounced Stalin. In Brecht's view, a change in the political situation could make a play better or worse. Its value depended on its usefulness in persuading the audience to initiate social change. Drama – like agitprop – should be didactic.

Whiting disagreed, but Kenneth Tynan, the *Observer*'s drama critic, was one of the leading pro-Brechtians, and he scoffed at the Old Vic lecture:

> It was an historic occasion. In the annals of the theatre, it may indeed come to be regarded as Romanticism's Last Stand, the ultimate cry of the artist before being engulfed by the mass, the final cry of individualism before being inhaled and consumed by the ogre of popular culture.

* Ronald Hayman 'A Last Interview with Brecht' *The London Magazine* vol 3 no 11 Nov 1956

He caricatured Whiting as an 'attenuated hermit saint bravely keeping his chin up while being sucked through the revolving doors of a holiday camp.'

Whiting may have been thinking of Tynan when he wrote in a notebook:

> The most dangerous tendency of modern criticism towards the work of young writers, especially in the theatre, is that it sets out to destroy by ridicule or abuse the writer's private mythology. Yet it is this private world which prevents the play becoming mere bombast, or journalism. If we are normal human beings, we live surrounded by terrors, clowns, dead loves and old fears, represented by, say, a painting on the wall, some reels of photographic negative, a rose garden and a call from another room. The artist, admitting their significance, naturally reaches out for them in the desperate urgency of creation. They are nothing in themselves, these material things, but what they evoke for us as writers matters very much.

The painting on the wall and the call from another room both feature in *Saint's Day*, while the reels of photographic negative appear in *Marching Song*, where Harry is described as a clown – a word used self-critically by both Hallam and Edward in *A Penny for a Song*.

What about the disagreement between Whiting and Tynan about the cultural crisis of the late Fifties? How does it appear in retrospect? If the audience at the Old Vic had been asked to express an opinion, the majority might have said Whiting was being too pessimistic. But would the same people still say so today?

In 1957, Margaret Thatcher had not yet been elected to parliament, but the government education policy was already trundling British people towards the point reached in 1998, when New Labour excluded the arts from the curriculum of state primary schools, and the BBC reduced the budgets of Radio 3 and Radio 4 to enrich Radio 1 and Radio 2. Unlike the playwright, the politician can address himself to a mass audience.

Some of Whiting's views about culture were in line with Friedrich Nietzsche's. Like Karl Marx, Nietzsche understood that education could be a powerful weapon in the hands of a state apparently trying to sharpen the intellectual acuity of its citizens and raise cultural standards, but really more concerned that voters should be uncritical. Unlike Marx, Nietzsche did not believe the dangers could be averted by democratising education. In an 1872 lecture he said: 'Universal education is only a preliminary for communism: education will in this way be so diluted as not to confer any privilege.'* He saw journalism as a means of disseminating culture in a diluted form. The only way people could be helped to enlightenment was through a more scrupulous and inspired use of language.

Whiting knew that clichés, slogans, jargon and imprecision in the use of language undermine precision in thinking and contribute to the process now generally known as 'dumbing down'. He never claimed he could help people to enlightenment, but his instinct was to use language carefully.

Some of the Fifties playwrights (such as John Arden) shied away from the word 'artist', as if all art were 'elitist'. Arden and many of the other Royal Court writers preferred to think of themselves as 'theatre workers'. The phrase 'political correctness' was not yet current in the Fifties, but it is not much more than a euphemism for 'conformism', and Whiting would have thought it absurd that the words *art* and *artist* should have acquired pejorative connotations. Caring deeply about the arts, especially literature, he had as much respect for literary tradition as for theatrical tradition.

Not that he was a conservative. Though he had not always voted, he had, as he says in 'Writer as Gangster', 'always mentally cast a vote for the Labour Party' until 1960. 'I say I am not committed. What I really mean is that I am not committed to any specific movement, because I find it extremely constricting. What some people overlook is that I have never written on any kind of social problem. I have always written on moral problems of a humanist kind, not of a religious kind.'

*Friedrich Nietzsche's 1872 lecture on 'The Future of Our Educational Institutions'.

Inevitably, his viewpoint was conditioned by the commercial failure of his plays, which showed that the cultural climate was unfavourable to a talent such as his. *A Penny for a Song, Saint's Day* and *Marching Song* had only brief runs in the West End, and the pieces in this book were all written before *The Devils* was staged. With the possible exception of Samuel Beckett, none of the playwrights who were enjoying greater success could be called better writers than Whiting, but he was rebuffed by the theatre, and for six years (1954-60) he wrote almost nothing for it.

It does not follow that what he wrote about it was embittered or unbalanced. What he said was just what needed to be said.

Ronald Hayman
London, 1998

A LECTURE

THE ART OF THE DRAMATIST

A LECTURE AT THE OLD VIC
(1957)

The art of the dramatist.

The first thing to be considered, I think, is this: the understanding on which a man writes plays today. I say today, because a consideration of how plays have been written in the past is a scholar's job, and must be left to another person at another time. So let me speak about what is going on today.

The first impression, and I think it is a true one, is that the arts are dying. Perhaps it would be better, more optimistic a beginning, to say that such a great change is taking place that what we knew as art is almost imperceptibly being replaced by something else. Of course, we go on pretending. The organisation for the continuance of the arts remain in existence: councils, critics, conferences and all the unproductive elements are doing well. Take a look at these, read their reports and reviews and you might think that the arts are in a healthy state of constant renewal.

But is this really so? No, it is not.

What then, you may ask, are all these exhibitions of paintings, these long publishers' lists, these concerts, these operas, these theatres? They are the remnants of a tradition: like the buttons on my sleeve.

A work of art is the statement of one man. It is one of the noblest, because it is one of the most selfless activities of human existence. It has nothing to do with an audience or a wish to please. It does not necessarily entertain, instruct or enlighten. It can do any one or all of these things, but that it should is not the artist's concern. That is the work of art in its perfect state. The thing is there: an audience taking from it what it can. It is not the artist's job to simplify the means of communication.

Communication. We hear a lot about it. Art is just that, we are told. Very well. Accept this proposition and you will find the most necessary equipment for the artist today is a public address system. So many people have to be reached now, all at the same level of comprehension and all at the same time. This has led to a degeneration. I suggest that the voice you hear today in all branches of literature including the theatre is not the individual voice but the collective voice. And this especially from any writer under forty. In other words, the writer has become the spokesman not for himself but for a group, an organisation, a class or a sect. The danger is that some don't know they are doing it, and those who do know often consider, and are led to consider it a virtue. 'This young man speaks for his generation.' 'This young woman is the rallying point for all young women with big feet.' You know the sort of thing.

The communal voice. We have settled for the time being and for better or for worse on the democratic life. We must hang together and speak as a man. But must we not consider that in these circumstances we shall have to give up what we call art? At least, in its conception of the past few hundred years. Why should we think that as an activity it is timeless? Why shouldn't this be the end? After all, like human life it is a fairly modern invention and neither are entirely satisfactory. Perhaps to make our days on earth longer we must also make them duller. And noisier. We must get through. We must be heard. We must communicate. One voice will never be enough. Call in the boys. And it is encouraged. It must be. Art has to conform to the conventions of life. It must also conform to its catchwords. Such as freedom. Freedom from authority, yes, it has that, apart from censorship. Freedom from the people? Certainly, it has freedom to speak just what they think. The cult of the individual is now almost as great a social crime in the West as it is a political crime in the East. This is unfortunate, as the cult of the individual is the basis of all art.

There are a few men, writers, composers, and painters, who in late middle and old age are continuing in the past tradition. It is this, I think, which gives the impression that all is as it was. The productions of a Picasso, an Eliot or a

Pound can still be measured by the critical apparatus used for their predecessors. And more important in this argument than the work they do is the way they set about doing it. But after them?

Has all artistic invention already dried up at source without our noticing it doing so behind the imposing screen of reprints of the classics, the National Gallery and the Shakespearean seasons?

Recently, whilst reading the arts pages of a respectable Sunday newspaper, I had a strange impression. It was this: that none of the plays and films seen, none of the books read, the paintings assessed or the music heard, had ever happened. I felt that all these, so remote from life did they seem, were the invention of the ladies and gentlemen responsible for the articles. Was it all, I wondered, a great conspiracy? My mind was partly set at rest a few days later when I saw one of the plays which had been reviewed. I say partly, because the play bore little or no resemblance to the play written about by the distinguished critic. However, it had the same title and some of the actors mentioned were there.

I have spoken of the older men. If I may speak of myself for a moment (I may do so in greater detail later) there are people of my age. Neither young nor old. Middle-aged. If we are lucky. Now, I grew up at a time in the 1930s when it was still believed that by the emancipation of the masses (I use the jargon of the time) a great new audience would be created for the arts. It was an old idea then, fifty years old at least, dating from Shaw and Morris. The sentimental Victorian picture of the poor but honest working man borrowing Ruskin from the public library still persisted. Raise his status and over the years he would be borrowing Spender, Auden, Malraux, Brecht and today, I suppose, that personification of public library reading, Colin Wilson. It was all quite natural. Men who were mad about drains wanted to give the depressed classes drains: artists wanted to give them art. I don't think it entered anyone's head at that time – certainly not in this country, although it may have occurred to a few cynical middle Europeans – that the status of art would be changed. That wasn't the idea at all. Anyway, the war and the years after the war brought about the change. The great mass of people were for the first time given a large measure of independence to choose. And did they use that choice in relation to the arts? No, they did not. Certainly, large numbers now subscribe to Beethoven and Tchaikovsky, performances of Shakespeare and colour prints of Van Gogh, but this isn't entirely what was intended. All that sort of thing is just museum going. The point is, the large mass of people reject any modern art as vigorously as ever. Why do they do this? I'll come to that later, and just say now that I believe they have excellent reasons.

What is known as the democratic way of life has changed the circumstances of the artist as completely as any totalitarian régime. The young men have realised that if they are to survive at all as artists and not just public entertainers they must recognise this and act accordingly. Hence, the collective voice. And the feeling that it is better than no voice at all. Which I suppose is true. The artist has always survived in spite of a society. The tactics used by the average Englishman have been to pretend that he was something else. He's never taken anyone in as far as I know. Certainly, he's never accepted as a gentleman. Equally, any young writer who imagines that by shouting about his working-class origins he is going to gain sympathy from that class is living in a fool's paradise. He can't have it both ways. He may walk down St James's Street in a bowler hat, or he may go to the seaside in a hat which is labelled 'Kiss Me Quick!' Either way he'll be found out. He'll never disguise that thing which the mass of people dislike and distrust – a creative ability. Why they dislike and distrust it has a psychological basis which would be out of place here.

And you must forgive this sociological-political preface to a talk which will very soon be about the art of the dramatist. It is important because it is the ground from which any art – either as we have known it in the past or what may have to pass for art in the future – must come. A dramatist, like any artist, draws his raw material from his time. And what is often misunderstood is that it cannot be other people's time. A young writer will be drawing on the personal experience of the past ten years. The years of the last war may mean very little to him. I, at my age, can draw on adult experience of twice that time, and the years of the war revealed more to me than any other period of my life. An older man can draw upon anything up to fifty or sixty years of observation and experience. What, then, is all this nonsense about an artist existing in his own time?

The questions are continually posed. What effect does the atom bomb have on writers today? What effect the Welfare State? Are we aware in our work of the extermination of the Jews in Europe during the war years?

Well, of course, anyone writing today is aware that these things happened and are happening. But it is the blind spot of the journalistic mind, so pre-eminent and so pre-occupied with art today, that it thinks the problems should be directly involved. In other words, the play must be set *in* a concentration camp, *beneath* an imminent explosion, or *in* a new town. The assumption seems to me naïve, but understandable. After all, the art of journalism, and a very fascinating and considerable art it is, must concern itself with the present happening in its exact place. But journalism is not the theatre or literature. Let me put it like this. Suppose a play is set in that uncontroversial place – an English drawing room. And the play is about – say, adultery. Suppose atom bombs, concentration camps and social welfare are never mentioned. And you know it's extraordinary how rarely they are in ordinary conversation. But this does not mean that they are not present or non-existent. The writer has been touched by these things, as we all have, and if the play is anything of a serious work it must be shadowed by them.

So I can come to the problem of what to write about.

And I shall consider it, for this is my subject, and I have reached it at last, on the level of writing for the theatre. The Art of the Dramatist.

At once I am in difficulties. I have no idea how playwrights go about their job. Except one. And that is myself. I have read letters and journals of writers in the past which give me an idea of their methods of work. I can often gather from these documents how many words were done in a day, what the weather was like, and who came to lunch. But how the play came to be written is usually very obscure, almost coyly avoided. If I turn to works of scholarship on the subject, I can find out the supposed source material of the play, and the influences on the writer at the time. But how it was done – well, the subject is avoided. In the simplest terms, of course, it is putting words on paper. But, as you will understand, something comes before and after that. If I look into books on How to Write a Play – I very rarely do, but I did before preparing this lecture – I find something which to me resembles the Highway Code. I feel I should understand it but don't. Of course, I think, that is very sensible: what a good idea: obviously the right way to do it. The only thing is, it seems to have nothing whatever to do with the work I have in hand. Rules are not much use to people like me, and I wonder if they are of any use to others.

So, as I warned you, I must speak largely from my own experience. That experience of playwriting falls into two parts. The first a period of some six years, during which four plays were written and staged. And a second period, the last three years, during which I have not written for the theatre but have come to certain conclusions on the subject of playwriting which may be of interest and which I am tentatively beginning to put into practice. Let me tell you of the practical experience of the first, and relate it to the theoretical reasoning of the second.

The subject of plays. What to write about. We are so often directed in this matter nowadays. Look at that! Isn't it iniquitous? Why don't you write about it? Corruption here! Why not expose it? Aren't you angry about this? You should put it in a play. All men of power, wealth and authority are blackguards: all poor, hardworking people are the children of

God. Or the other way round. It doesn't really matter. Get down to 'real' life. Let me explain this. I must quote from a recent article: 'And at the same discussion it became clear that when most people (Mr John Whiting objecting) urge that plays should be about "life" (in inverted commas) and about "people" (also in inverted commas) they mean plays about sociological life and about working-class people.' End of quote.

Now do you know why Mr John Whiting objected? (It was very quietly done: just by silence, if I remember rightly.) Perhaps you will when I tell you how I have come to write plays.

I have written a play from remembering a gratuitous act of cruelty which I committed when I was a child. I have written another from a sudden moment of understanding on seeing a man's face during a war trial. He was not working class. He was a soldier. And he was a person. I have written a comedy for no better reason, and is there a better reason, than to make a friend laugh.

These 'things given' are the starting point. Many, of course, are rejected. Perhaps they are unsuitable for plays. Perhaps they bore me, and I can't stand the thought of spending nearly a year of my life dealing with them. Sometimes an incident, a theme, will go out of my mind. I shall forget it completely. And this is very important. You forget things, almost unconsciously put them aside. But they come back. At moments of personal crisis. Moments which have nothing to do with work. On a day when I feel I wouldn't care if I never wrote another word or saw another play. Yet that can be the very moment which begins the play.

This is one of the reasons why I've never been able to look upon myself as a proper writer. Many writers, I'm told, can sit down happily day after day and write. It is their job. No nonsense about that. Three thousand words today, they say, note it in their journal and go out for a walk. Do they really do this? Lucky men.

Very well. I have had an idea. I have forgotten it. Then this sometimes absurdly trivial incident occurs. It may be seeing some girl in a restaurant: it may be getting frighteningly lost in a foreign city: or getting drunk. It may be very important, something to change the whole life, such as the death of a friend. Anyway, it happens and the lost idea recurs. It comes back. Subtly invested with a significance it never had before. The impulse at once is to translate it into an attempted work of art. In my case, a play. The intellectual notion and the happening in life breed. Sometimes in an odd way. The pretty girl who smiled in the bookshop may give birth to a political tragedy. The dying friend to farce.

Now, the question I want to ask, and I'm going to make no attempt to answer it, is this: is such a method hopelessly outdated? Should we not take our material directly from life, as a journalist does, and attempt to impose on it the shape which will make it a work of art? In other words, don't people want the facts in the theatre as in other forms today, and to hell with any personal slant on the subject? These are questions I shall leave you to answer.

All dramatic works have a point round which all action is formed. It need not be a moment of theatre, of effect; in fact it should not be. It may never be apparent to audiences, it may never be discovered in hundreds of years by scholars. It may never even be known to the actors, although if they're good ones they'll smell it out. The good ones have a nose for that sort of thing. This dramatic point is the 'thing given', the first idea which I've talked about translated into the play. It may now be a line of dialogue, or a silence, or a moment of action. It is not necessarily the ultimate point of the play. I mean, it need not come at a climactic moment in the last act. It forms the point of departure for the writer. He may work towards it, he may work away from it. Embracing it, as might be said with the development. This point, of which the writer is most aware, is the germ of the structure of the play. Now, theatre time is elastic: a play can be written which covers thousands of years – it has been written – or it can be contained within a few hours. The placing of this crucial incident which I have mentioned is the first step in the physical structure of the play. Do you follow me? Working on the assumption that the play is of a finite length, say two hours, then it must be decided within the action how much will lead to the crucial moment and how much will lead from it. In short, how much comes before and how much after it.

This is a fundamental point. It has nothing to do with fashion, so there can be no question except of an academic kind.

Let's get on.

Now the play will begin to be seen. And the action will begin to be seen against some kind of background. It may, depending on the play – it should never depend upon the whim of the producer – be a real place, a room, a garden, what we call a naturalistic setting. I have never used anything but this. I find, as yet, that I'm unable to use the stage as a platform. Merely a place. Although this is a perfectly valid usage, in my opinion.

So the setting of the play begins to be seen.

When I was a child, about twelve, I suppose, and first began to go to the theatre, it made a considerable impression on me. But in a very limited way. For a long time I saw all art and a large part of life in theatrical terms. In painting I was attracted by the high lit drama of a Latour or a Martin. In music it was always a distant trumpet call, a side drum, and, delicious sensation, a human voice speaking absolute nonsense but with music. Tremulo strings, if possible. In the theatre it was The Moment. That marvellous moment in Act Two when so-and-so did such-and-such. Indeed, after many years I can remember such marvellous moments but I can't for the life of me tell you what the play was about. Anyway, this seems to me now a very infantile way of seeing the theatre. Yet it persisted for a long time, long enough to influence the first plays I wrote.

More important, I saw life in these curious terms of highly lit moments. And most important of all, I saw myself in such a way.

Now, when the art, the man and the material are all seen in these theatrical terms, the result, if nothing else, should be theatrical. And they are. And that, at the risk of sounding wilful, is wrong. I suggest that the theatrical has no place in the theatre today. This virtuosity, with people dropping dead at just the right moment, these cadenzas: I reject them. I must. They don't even touch me anymore when I see them in the theatre. The little frame, the small lighted box, which to me was, and for many people is, the theatre is untrue. There is no other work of art of which we applaud the detail, unless we're trying to make kind excuses. Everyone must have experienced that long silence in front of a painting when no one can think of anything to say. We stare at the canvas in misery: yes, there is a river, some swans, a distant church, bad weather coming up. The silence goes on until at last one brave man asks brightly the only question possible. Where is it? We are always asking that of the theatre, of the play.

I would like to approach the theatre in future with a great austerity. I am a little sad about this because I have a strong inclination towards the baroque theatre. And on a pure level of enjoyment I love the theatre at its silliest: Lehar, and that sort of thing. But all that is part of the museum now.

When I say austere I don't mean bare stages with actors chanting hieratical drama. I mean rather a greater sense of truth. Not naturalism. The sense of truth which makes plays of apparent fantasy such as *Fin de Partie* and *The Chairs* more moving and more truthful than the examples of neo-realism and social significance we get offered in the English theatre.

Even so, I can think of no pure examples in the theatre anywhere. But there are two in the cinema, both films by the same man. Bresson's *Diary of a Country Priest,* and *A Man Has Escaped*. These films state the facts of a situation, they are made against the dramatic line, they avoid the moment of theatre, and by doing so become intensely exciting.

Here is another question for you. Has the whole business of entertainment become so large, so much a struggle for effect, that it is now the artist's job no longer to invent, to use his imagination, to interpret, but only to state? The facts. Just put down on paper, on a stage, on film, the facts.

Very well. The play has a place and a time. Now all plays concern themselves with men and women, or at least, with human behaviour, even if only in reflection. (I am thinking of those rather rare plays with a cast of animals, gods or insects. And even Wagner found it impossible to depersonalise the characters in *The Ring* when it came to the practical job of writing.) It is wrong to believe that the characters of a play *are* the play, that they make up the play. It is an easy mistake to make, because the people in a play are the most easily and immediately comprehensible factor. But, in fact, the play is formed by circumstances reacting on character. Plays are not, or should not be, just about very interesting people.

In the past, before beginning to write a play the characters have presented themselves to me. I mean, I have never had to search for people to act out the play. I have a title and a list of characters before a word of the play is written and, as yet, I have never had to add or subtract from them. They have arrived like a well-mannered cast on the morning of the first rehearsal to play their part. Just the right number.

This is something I would not change.

There is something called 'taking people from life'. This has always mystified me. Where else can you take them from? You can take ideas from art, but not people. They have been observed, sometimes subconsciously, sometimes at a distance, sometimes closely and without any real intention of using them as material for a play. I don't think anyone goes around with a notebook, like a bird watcher. So you have them immediately below the title, if you have a title, of the play. As yet they are unnamed. Thought of as the man who does this, and the woman who does that. They are like strangers seen in the street. They already have surface characteristics, but little which makes them individual. They will stay like this until the writing of the play.

There is something about naming characters which may be mentioned here. They begin as people whose faces you know, but whose names you don't. So you give them names, tentatively at first; they shift, and even the final decision is uneasy at first. It's like having a new child in the house. It has been named, but the name has nothing to do with a personality because there is no personality. The name seems cumbersome, even pretentious, for such nothingness. But in a little while a personality begins, characteristics show and the name – well, it seems impossible that the person could be called anything else. I mention this because the naming of characters is perhaps their first real identity in the play.

So: there is a theme: there is a place: and there are people.

The writing can begin. Now, I don't think I am being over-sensitive when I say that this act, this decision to begin, is as disgusting and horrible as committing a murder. In one's mind there is the pure ideal, the perfect crime, as you might say. Yet from the moment you pick up the pen you know that you're not going to get away with it. At best, you can hope to have a very good try. Everything has been planned, you know where everyone will be at any one time: you are fairly sure what they will say at any given situation. Fine. You'll get away with it, ending superbly confident, innocent and successful. What happens in fact? Very little that was planned. The characters in taking on life take on initiative. Now when you're young and beginning to write this can seem very exciting. This spontaneous action appears to be the very fount of inspiration, and it can, I admit, produce these moments of theatre which I now deplore. But it does not produce good plays. I see plays nowadays by young writers and I sometimes think, 'Oh dear, if only he'd cut out all the "good bits".' When you get older you learn to cut back this irresponsible behaviour of the characters. You tell them to shut up. That you're not concerned with their miserable self-pitying outpourings and their pathetic attempts at humour, and by doing so you begin to get some sort of shape.

We still hear talk about the well-made play. Dramatists don't often talk about it, but others do. No one has ever defined what a well-made play is. I take it to be something of this kind. A play which is like a satisfying conjuring trick, which clicks open and shut at the right moment. Which in action is just a fraction behind the audience's apprehension all the way along. In other words, the audience is expecting the leading man of the company, the star, to come through that door at any moment. He does come through that door. Splendid. Applause. Or the audience knows something that the actors pretend not to know. It is revealed. Astonished actors. Clever audience. When I was a child and went to the pictures the villain always seemed to be creeping up on the hero. And when he did this a shout would go up from the front rows: 'Look out! He's behind you!' I always think of the well-made play as 'Look out! He's behind you!' plays. Let's ignore them.

But a play must have structure or, like anything else, it wouldn't exist. What is often misunderstood is that dramatic structure is not something which can be discussed and evaluated on its own. The structure of a play is composed of the elements which make the play itself. The spoken word, the story and the action of that story. And there is no one way of doing it. Every structure will depend on the diversity of these elements.

Let me give you an example. The libretto of Verdi's opera *Otello*, which was taken from the Shakespeare play, is on this level of criticism a better dramatic structure than the original play. It is shorter, more concise, more dramatic, and the characters of both Iago and Othello are much less ambiguous. Now are we going to say that Boito was a better dramatist than Shakespeare? I think it's doubtful. Yet the total work of the opera is a masterpiece of the theatre. You can see the difficulties which immediately present themselves when this form of criticism is applied.

I have said that the spoken word is one of the elements which form the dramatic structure. In the theatre it is also the main factor in forming the characters. The kind of language which is used. It is very difficult to see a point where the play can dispense with language. If it does so it changes its identity and becomes mime or ballet. Language must be considered an indispensable part of drama.

One of the reasons for the decline in dramatic writing is the shift, actually the debasement, of language which has happened towards the middle of this century. An age which can talk in all seriousness of 'a peace offensive', refer to an intercontinental ballistic missile as 'a defensive weapon' and as a practical possibility speak of 'a democratic monarchy' is not one of the easiest to communicate with on the level of pure sense. There are instances today, as Mr Eliot has pointed out, when a writer may be misunderstood because he is saying exactly what he means. Even if he manages to communicate, there is the further hazard that what he says will then be translated into what the audience wishes him to say. Some years ago now, when one of my plays was produced in London, the *Daily Worker* hailed me as a man with a true sympathy for the condition of my fellow men: for the same play the *Evening Standard* came near to calling me a fascist.

Probably the true art of the dramatist is this art of the spoken word. And, as I have said, it is the most difficult problem today. With the spoken word the dramatist forms his characters, his play and so communicates with his audience. The writing of a play is concerned with finding these words.

The simplest way of communicating with people is to speak their jargon. Now, it is not easy to communicate ideas to someone even on the same level of understanding. It is easier in some things than others, of course. Everyone must have experienced the ease with which they can tell someone how much they hate them, and the difficulty in truly telling someone how much they love them. Again, society in this country is divided into classes by types of language more surely than by any other thing. I don't mean by accents. I mean by vocabulary and usage. Not only does each class have its own usage but also each generation. It might be said that today we are a polyglot nation. You will understand the difficulty to a writer.

The difficulty exists in all literature today. But in the theatre it is bedevilled by a further consideration. The theatre deals in the spoken word. Now, no one has as yet found a satisfactory way of recording human speech by words on paper. By transcribing it, exactly. When it is done as accurately as possible the reader, even if it be the original speaker, will transform them. Today the most acceptable form of language in the theatre it would seem is the direct unornamented speech of everyday life. Acceptable to an audience, I mean. But what is this direct unornamented speech? Pick up a conversation in the street and it may go something like this:

'Now look here I said I'm not having this I said and so he says What and I says I'm not having it I'm telling you I says up and down the stairs you were four times this morning telling him I was up and down I says in your boots with little Else trying to sleep oh I told him.'

No, the direct unornamented speech of the theatre must be as artificial as any form.

In the early days of playwriting I thought my job was to use language to the best of my ability, not in its plain form but as a poet uses it. For one thing I was concerned with beauty in those days, a hangover from the English lyric tradition. And I was concerned with all the tricks of the trade such as forming words into musical sound, making them pointed and, if possible, witty.

At my last play a man sitting behind me suddenly said in an irritable way: 'But people don't talk like this.' Well, of course, I know people don't talk in such a way. I was only following a tradition that it was the writer's job, and what is more his prerogative, to invent language. The words of Shakespeare's plays are not the words of the Elizabethan people of England.

Now I believe that all language for the theatre should be taken from life. It is no longer permissible to invent. This means the concern will not only be for the highly articulate man using words with care and for effect, but also with the idiot mumblings of the half-wit who lives down the lane.

What people are and what people do. This seems to me the absolute function of the play now. To show this with no ornamentation. To leave the poetry out of the words: to rigidly refuse all which is for effect.

Perhaps you think that would make a dull play. Then may I ask you to consider this? Are you more deeply touched, moved and amused by happenings in life or in the theatre? Surely in everyday life. Yet the incidents in life rarely contain literary poetry, and God is the clumsiest stage manager ever when it comes to the telling effect.

However, with theme, place, time and people, the play comes to be written, no matter what kind. Written and rewritten, for as in every form, I believe it is this going over which gives the final significance. The continual taking away to reveal the absolute work. Yet even about this I'm not sure.

Recently, at a cocktail party, I was talking or trying to talk to one of the runners-up in the *Observer* play competition.* I was making heavy going with him. I grasped at a conversational straw which floated past. I asked: did it take you long to write your play? He treated the fatuous question in the way it deserved. He looked kindly at me: he had no idea who or what I am: he shook his head. No, he said, I just took April off and wrote it. Well, if any of you are thinking of taking April off to write a play, what I have been saying to you must seem the most precious kind of academic tightrope walking.

It would be fine if it could be said how it was done, this writing of a play. Some people are presumptuous enough to say more: they will tell you how it *should* be done. How long it takes to do, how and on what level it is written, the style, the technique, the degree of know-how, all these are matters of individual opinion.

The only constant factor is the fantastic task the dramatist sets out to do. Think of it. The culmination to the writing and

*Held in 1956.

staging of a play. It is the gathering together of many hundred people in one place and at the same time. They come singly or in the smallest groups, strangers to each other. One will be suffering from indigestion, another will have quarrelled with his wife, one's feet hurt, another, perhaps young, has been struck in Shaftesbury Avenue with a sudden vision of the supreme happiness of human life which no mere playwright can hope to match. So they come in – some of them late – and it is the playwright's job – nothing less – to weld these thousand disparate beings into an attentive whole. It is very difficult not to resort to trickery to succeed in this. For it can be done by the tricks which I, for one, know very well. But is this what it's all about? Is the whole thing just a confidence trick on a not very credulous public? The danger of the confidence trick is that it becomes known and as time goes on fewer and fewer people are taken in by it. And at last the trickster is driven towards honesty for his living. He has to become one with other people.

And when all is said and done, that is what a dramatist must finally do with his audience. I said earlier that he should not be aware of them as an audience whilst writing the play. But he must be aware of them as people.

Am I wrong in thinking that audiences, and especially young audiences, today won't accept the theatre because of its death's-head artificiality? I think it's true. People no longer want to be taken out of themselves, as the saying was, because now they are themselves and are aware of how good a thing that is.

Two institutions are notably in decline these days: the Arts and the Church. And both for the same reason. They are practising an abracadabra which takes in no one. The feeling is that both artists and the Church are trying to trick people into accepting something which is worthless. The sales talk, the little free packets of wisdom we both give away, quite obscure the fact that both the Church and the Arts have something real to offer.

TWO INTERVIEWS

WRITER AS GANGSTER

An Interview with John Whiting by the Editors of *Encore,*
Clive Goodwin and Tom Milne*
(1961)

You were once an actor, weren't you?

Yes, I was. I went to RADA, and had to call myself
something between 1937 and 1939, when I went into the army.
In 1945 I came out, and was completely at a loss what to do.
I had no money at all, so I went back to acting. I was at
Harrogate for about a year, and then eventually at York for
three years, where I began to write plays.

Was your experience as an actor of much use to you as a playwright?

Yes, I think so. In fact, I don't suppose I'd ever have written
plays if I hadn't been an actor. After the army I wrote a certain
amount of other things. I wrote a short book about the war. It
wasn't any good, but I showed it to somebody and he said,
'Why don't you write plays? It seems extraordinary that you,
an actor, don't write for the theatre.' So I sat down and wrote
Saint's Day. I did write a play before that, but it didn't work out
very well. Recently I rewrote it as a television play. The critics
said, 'What on earth is he doing? He's forty something and
he's writing like a twenty-eight year old.' They were dead right,
of course. I changed a good deal, but I couldn't get away from
the basic thing.

You do attend rehearsals of your plays?

I do on most of the plays – less so now, because I find
there's nothing I can do. I used to sit – a sort of dummy at
the back. I never had ambitions to become a second producer:
most of the directors I've worked with would have been
put out if I had.

How do you actually write?

I write in longhand. I used to write on sheets of paper, but
now I write in a black leather notebook which I carry around

---

*Priced originally at a shilling, *Encore* was started at the end of 1954 as 'a
quarterly magazine for students of the theatre'. Its readership soon widened,
it became bi-monthly, and its contributors included many of the most
important men and women of the theatre. It survived till the mid-sixties.

with me. I find that I can't write in one place any more, and for the past eighteen months or so I've been on the move almost continually. My writing time on plays is comparatively small – the actual time I sit with a pen in my hand, that is. When I began writing, because I was miserably unsure of what I was doing, I used to make a dozen drafts. I'm a totally uneducated person, with no academic education at all... well, I was at a public school, but I never passed an exam, and I didn't go to university. This shows sometimes. Nowadays, I prepare more. I manage a play in two, maybe three drafts. I write a draft, then a revised draft, then I type, then I correct, then I type a script. From that point onwards it's a question of revision. This is something I find rather difficult – the problem is to recreate the mental and emotional climate in which I wrote the thing originally. I'm often apt to get stuck over technical problems, and the thing goes cold on me. The pen I use was presented to me by the Critics' Circle in 1957.

I think I've heard you say before now that Saint's Day *was a purely personal exercise.*

Um!... a technical exercise as well. I think everybody writes one play on which he then draws technically for the rest of his life. You have on paper a sort of anthology of what you can do.

Can you say what the generation of Saint's Day *was – the starting point of the play? An incident, a character?*

It was a place, actually, and a mural in a house. A place where I was in the army – which is probably the reason for the presence of the soldiers in the play. It was in the early part of the war, in the Midlands somewhere. It was winter and it was miserable. We had nothing to burn so we went out to see if we could find a house we could tear down. In quite large grounds we came across this obviously derelict house. We went in, there were no lights, and we had to use torches. And *there* was this most extraordinary painting on the wall.

Roughly as you describe it in the play? Five standing figures, a dog and a figure to be filled in?

No, not the dog. That's where I began to invent. But how *do* these things start? I don't know. Standing there in that house, I suddenly had the most extraordinary feeling, which stayed with me for six years. Then I reached back on it.

Was the house the way you describe it in the play?

Yes. It was actually a Victorian house, but it had a Victorian Gothic thing about it. And the iron balcony was outside the room.

In the preface to the plays, you say, 'The so-called symbolism of Saint's Day *is no more than the use of people, places, things, even ideas and quotations from literature which have a personal significance put together to form a whole'. Now, the five figures in the mural probably have a personal significance, but the figure that was unspecified takes on a kind of symbolism, at the end of the play when the dead body of Stella is used as a model to complete it. Again, perhaps there is gratuitous symbolism when the child from the village appears at the very end of the play, and by a strange coincidence is also called Stella. Isn't this symbolism?*

Yes, I suppose so. Perhaps, really, it's a kind of trickery. A very simple form of trickery. I don't see any reason why one shouldn't use a form of significant coincidence. You do it in poetry, and in painting. It's like people saying nobody talks in poetry. They don't. But that doesn't invalidate it as a form. Therefore, I don't see any reason why one shouldn't use a perfectly blatant form of coincidence. You can use it like that because it's a shock, it's over, finished. It wouldn't be possible to base a long sequence of events on such a coincidence.

What you're saying is, because it's theatrical, because it takes place instantly in the theatre, it's legitimate? There's another very good example in the play. Stella's premonition of disaster when she says, 'Careful, we are approaching the point of deviation... the call from another room'. And this call from another room comes when Stella is killed.

Yes. That, of course, is a parody of Eliot. This is what I mean when I say it was an enormous exercise. Because people never believe me when I say that I never expected the play to be done. Knowing the English theatre as I'd done for the past ten or twelve years, I thought it was extremely remote that anybody would actually stage the play. But I thought it was very well worth writing, to see what I could do. And I used all sorts of literary devices and tests such as parody and memories. *A Penny for a Song,* which was my next play, was a sort of *jeu d'esprit,* something one was amused to write. The whole thing swings to another extreme in *Marching Song.* Everything is pared down technically.

Would you make a distinction between, say, Saint's Day *and* Marching Song, *on the one hand, which seem to be packed with thought and meaning, and* Penny for a Song *and* Gates of Summer *on the other?*

Ye... es. You see, *Penny for a Song* is rather clumsy in its structure but it's a better play than any of the others, curiously enough. It has a much lighter texture, but it *is* the best play of the three. *Marching Song* is not a successful play – it's much too dense.

That's not necessarily a criticism of the play.

I think so. It's like an over-scored piece of music. I could have done it with far less of both resources and material. There are pieces of music like this. It's got a thickened sense about it. It suffers slightly from a kind of intellectual elephantiasis.

But you have at one time said that a work of art was not something which was thrown to the masses – it was for a kind of intellectual elite. Surely with a play like Saint's Day *or* Marching Song, *which is packed because of the tremendous complexity of the allusions, you ought to expect the audience which you write for to pick up those references even though the wider audiences do not?*

The point about *Marching Song* is that its arguments are absolutely valid, it's watertight on its level of human behaviour, and on its argument. This is all splendid, but I don't think it's successful as a play. It's too enclosed. It's too much of a conversation piece. Too shut in. It needs to be opened out. And of course it's glacial on a human level. The sex business with Forster coming back to Catherine, and the girl. It doesn't work because they're frozen to death before they can develop. And I could never do anything with it. The whole thing is weighted so heavily on one side. There is Forster, the soldier, and Cadmus the Chancellor, who don't exist below the eyes, they're simply all head. On the other side the only person who's more than that, who comes towards any reasonable sort of humanity, is a fool like Lancaster, the film director. The girl is terribly cold. She, too, reasons – picks it up like an infectious disease.

She's very cool, beat almost? And this was in 1954. She's now really very representative.

She was created out of a number of people I had seen and talked to in Europe immediately after the war. I planned the play about 1948. I wrote it in 1951.

How did you come to write it?

Oh, I was just fascinated by the subject. The war criminals and so on. And I drew on people I knew before the war – a professional soldier I knew in the German army for Forster. It all fascinated me very much, and the elements came together.

Your criticism of the play's coldness, have you always felt this?

No I didn't think it at the time. I came to it after going over it and working on other things. Many people thought the original production lacked warmth, but that was the way I wanted it. The same goes for Robert Flemyng's performance. I admired it very much but it wasn't moving – it wasn't supposed to be.

Do you feel you're more successful along these lines in A Penny for a Song, *for example?*

This is very difficult because people often insist that the level of communication on which I fail is on what they call a human level, and this isn't very understandable to me because I'm not quite sure what they mean. I have an instinctive horror of sentimentality. I find it extremely difficult to humanise, because I am, I suppose – well, I am an absolute sucker for B pictures, and will have a good cry. I know this you see, and I know the extraordinary danger in writing – what immense effect can be obtained by a downpour of hot treacle. And therefore – although this is probably overstating it a little – I swing the other way. I suspect the term happiness, which is used a great deal. I recognise that it does exist, of course, but I suspect it as a form of argument, or as a point of departure. I really don't think that the theatre is just a place where people should laugh or cry – as was said to me only recently by someone whose opinion I respect. I do not necessarily believe that they should think too much. I don't think *that*. It is the oversimplification. I mean, in this wonderful savage, barbaric age – people insist on talking in terms of strawberries and cream.

Talking of strawberries and cream, isn't this something of the effect one gets from A Penny for a Song, *and to a lesser extent from* Gates of Summer *?*

I should have said that *The Gates of Summer* was the harshest play I've ever written. Don't fall into the common error of believing that laughter is kind.

A side question. You always have intriguing names for your characters, laden with significance, somehow. Christian Melrose, for example. Why Christian?

I don't know. People *are* called Christian.

Procathren, Catherine de Troyes?

Well, any name *can* be laden with significance. You take an early Ionesco play, which called everybody Smith, Jones and Robinson or something. By virtue of calling them Smith, Jones and Robinson, he immediately attached significance to those names. I think you can do it with almost anything. People said it about *Marching Song*. I like a sort of euphony, and before I start a play, I run through the names to make certain that the Christian names or the surnames are not all one, two or three syllables. Dido, Catherine, Rupert, John, Harry – so that you get a sort of pattern. Or if you have Fred, Jim, Bill – you get a pattern in the same way because they *are* all the same. I don't think there's any greater significance to my use of names than that.

You probably lay a false trail by using Catherine de Troyes *and* Dido, *perhaps quite accidentally.*

Yes, I know. And *Cadmus,* too. I was faced with a problem in that play, of course, because I didn't want to use names like Von Runstedt, Von Manstein, and so on. Do you see what I mean? Therefore, I chose a name like Forster, which is found in Germany, applicable in France, and is found in England, and the same thing with the Christian names, which are interchangeable in most European countries.

It was interesting that when Saint's Day *was first performed at the Arts, its defenders were mostly theatrical people who said, 'This play kicked me in the stomach. It's marvellous', whereas everybody else was sitting around saying, 'What the hell is it about?' This is perhaps the density of the texture again. In performance the play gives a sort of picture of what you're saying; only later does one analyse it and pick up references like 'the point of deviation'. These things tie up marvellously when you have time to think about them, but of course, they do work in the theatre in an imaginative way. Would you say that a play like* Saint's Day *should be approached as a kind of imaginative statement rather than a logical argument?*

Yes, you see, I construct on a sort of thematic basis, almost a subconscious thing, whereby words gain a significance – a word like hat, or house – to the characters within the play. This is the texture of the play, and it doesn't seem to me to be frightfully important that an audience should recognise it. It's merely a method of writing. I've got to find some way of putting the wretched stuff down on paper. This happens to be my way. Now, what happens is that if ever I am fool enough to say to an actor or a director, 'Don't you see my dear fellow because she says *hat* here, and he says *hat* there...', then they are on to it, and I, as playwright, am lost. It's like saying of a building, 'How very extraordinary about this brick, it's not only supporting, it's being supported...' and suddenly you get into an argument which doesn't matter at all. All you need to do is to open the door and go into the house: that's what it's for. You see what I mean? It's this danger of over-investigation, because this is only a method, it isn't a significance within the thing itself. The significance is the total and overall effect, not these methods – and everybody, obviously, has different methods. The method, for example, which takes significant incidents and joins them together. I can't do that. I have to work on a sort of musical shape.

This is quite conscious?

Oh, yes.

A specific example: The trees used in the hanging at the end of Saint's Day *are mentioned casually at several points earlier in the play, giving them a sort of personality. Did you think, 'I'm going to use these trees for the hanging at the end, so I'll introduce them earlier'?*

Yes, because I knew where I was going. I knew what the end of play was going to be. And therefore you prepare, you indicate – but it's not necessary. You appeal to a lower level than the immediate consciousness of any member of the audience. You see what I mean? A character mentions 'Trees' and it's gone, because someone is saying something else about breakfast or stairs or trumpets or soldiers or clergymen. But there's an accumulated thing within the comparatively short time you spend in the theatre – an accumulation of ideas – (I'm taking the fact for granted that the audience is paying attention to the play and is of reasonable intelligence) and your total effect at the end is what residue you have left. Many people will miss some points – but analysis in performance is exactly like the over-criticism of music. The subscription of the flute at a certain bar is not important but it is often picked out. It's not important – it could well be forgotten. It's the total effect which matters.

But you can't really make your effect without the flute.

No, no, because if you begin to cut these things, you haven't got a play. There's always this terrible problem when one sits down, and writes at the top of the page 'Act One'. You think, 'Now I know what I'm going to do,' and then you think, 'What are they going to say?' Take *The Devils,* for example. The story is elementarily simple. A rakish and libertine priest of great charm, high intelligence – well, he wasn't but I've made him so – he has his women, he has power, he's handsome, reasonably rich, and up at the convent there's this lunatic, this crazy mother who suddenly begins to have terrible ideas that Beelzebub is lodged in her stomach, or in her lower bowel, or something like that and is speaking with the voice of the priest. The situation is simply that local superstition, politics, fear, revenge, all subscribe to the fact that people come to believe it, and he's arrested, tried and burned. Now, that's all it is. Well, I mean this could all be put down on half a page. But the thing is a play – somebody's got to say something, and therefore one has got to find the significant points in it, and a shape. Where do you start? Well, I've started in the gutter, I mean literally in the gutter, and the play gets up out of it. That's the overall shape, but how do you do it? You have to do it by a series of steps. Now these steps again are not important, except to the very few people who want to know how these things are written. The public's not concerned with the finesse of making a play or a chair or anything else. It merely wants a serviceable article which will do a certain thing – and that can be anything – it can frighten them, or stimulate them or work them into a frenzy of rage: all these things are perfectly permissible.

Have you ever found that criticism has been useful to you?

Yes. I'm more humble than people give me credit for.

I mean when your first play Saint's Day *was produced at the Arts, it was greeted by a howl of derision, it really was...*

Well of course, I didn't get any criticism out of that. I didn't get anything I could possibly use. Had one calm voice spoken up out of that hullabaloo... but there really wasn't one, not one. Harold Hobson called me a lunatic, and so it went on. The only beginning was about a year after it was done in London, when Peter Hall produced it at Cambridge, and out of the university began to come the first comprehensible criticism. It was not all good – I mean they didn't all say, 'This is a marvellous play which has been wronged'. They said, 'As a matter of fact this is not a very good play, but there is this that and the other'. And gradually criticism began to be written which I could start to read as if it meant something.

Did the Arts reception make you feel that you'd got into the wrong profession, or did you feel that it was 'their' fault?

Oh, I thought it was their fault.

But you didn't at any time have sufficient – er – respect for the critics to feel that their opinion was valid and you really were a punk writer?

Oh, No! No! No! I suppose there have been people who have actually given up the theatre and not written any more plays because the critics have said they couldn't do it. People have always said that I can't do it. I can't, probably. But I do. That's the point. It's a sort of compulsive thing. I did give it up – I mean I didn't write a play for six years. Partly because I do find the theatre basically a terribly unsatisfactory thing to write for, especially as I get older.

You wrote Gates of Summer *in 1953?*

I completed the first draft just before *Marching Song* was put on.

And then – for six years – you wrote primarily for films?

Yes, but I did begin two plays. I wrote half of one. It was hopeless, it wouldn't work at all. I put it away, and I started another one, of which again I wrote half. A very fascinating subject. Couldn't ever work, never worked, boring beyond words, so I put that away. It was only recently that I realised that the first play I started is perfectly all right. I've just changed the place and I've changed the basic idea. lt was simply that I was writing the wrong play, that's all.

Why was it the wrong play? Was it because you were not expressing yourself accurately?

I don't know. I don't know. It's only in recent years that I've been prepared to commit myself on any very definite opinions about things. I used to hedge. I suffer very much from being able to see both sides of the question. I suppose it's because of my age, and coming out of the late thirties, and then the war and... I don't know. I no longer bother. I'm so prepared to leave so many things to other people now. Whereas before so many things were expected of me, social things. You know it's very interesting that in all the plays I have written there's nothing whatsoever to indicate my party politics, nothing – as opposed to somebody, like say, Arnold Wesker or Robert Bolt, who are quite outspoken in such matters. I have never, for example, put down in any of the plays in print, at any point, my attitude towards certain present problems, like nuclear disarmament. I have never used any terms of religion in the plays, except as expletives. *Marching Song,* for example, is a play in which one might think, somebody somewhere would mention God, but nobody ever does. And yet a complete picture is often formed of exactly what I am. Now this is very interesting, you see, because in actual fact it isn't as simple as that. Beliefs are what one basically is, and what one writes from. But people like Wesker – the last time I talked to him – obviously thought I was nothing at all, that I had achieved a marvellous situation of being quite non-partisan, except for occasional snarls, and that I didn't exist with either foot on the ground.

If some sort of standpoint didn't come out of your plays, I don't think we'd be interested in them.

No, no, but you see, I don't use political philosophy or religious philosophy or any form of social philosophy as arguments. In the way that Brecht does, for example – he uses communism as a form of argument in nearly all the later plays. But I don't do that. This certainly doesn't invalidate the fact that one obviously has to have a point of view. Frankly, all the writers I most admire in Europe are the disengaged writers.

You would describe yourself as a disengaged writer?

Oh yes, entirely. Disengaged from what? Not from life itself – I mean, I lead a reasonable sort of life, it's rather untidy, but I do most of the things most people do and make the same mistakes. I don't think that because you say you are disengaged you are necessarily ivory-tower. I think you can, of course, be disengaged and remote, but it's becoming more and more apparent that the artist is proving to be a failure as a propagandist, and therefore I think he must go back to being something more basic. He's obviously got a job, and he'll have a job in any form of society, but you see propaganda has methods. People do talk about art as propaganda, but to me living in the 30s, for example, and knowing Europe, there are many many more efficient methods of propaganda than art – then why not use them? Don't write a play about it, use one of the propaganda methods. This is what I really mean. I think art's a useless instrument of propaganda, that's why I entirely disagree with Brecht. And anyway, I'm right and he's wrong, that's obviously been proved because his plays are not good propaganda. They're good plays, the later ones, but not good propaganda.

Isn't it a question of degree in what you mean by propaganda?

The word has come to have social overtones and also implies an attempt at didacticism – it means you're trying to teach people the right thing or what you believe to be right.

But surely any good play is doing that. In Saint's Day *you're making a kind of statement?*

No, no, it does it by something else. It does it by a method of revelation. It doesn't do it by a method of direct teaching. That's the point. That's when the theatre can come in line with other arts. It's extremely difficult to paint propaganda pictures, as Picasso, for example, has found. I mean, most propaganda symbols are bad art, like the Union Jack. As a Communist, Picasso is sometimes called upon, and sometimes very much wishes, to paint what you might call propaganda. This presents a great problem. I mean, he can paint a symbol like a dove which can then be used the world over as a symbol. But this isn't actual propaganda; he's not really doing anything, he might have taken anything. It has its effect simply because it happens to be painted by Picasso. The theatre can do this too, but it has got to be done through a form of revelation: it can't be done by a direct statement. And this is where people go wrong nowadays.

Recently, writing in The London Magazine, *you quoted Thomas Mann's 'A work of art is something which is worth doing for its own sake.' This I would doubt.*

Now this is very difficult because, take it to its extreme and we're back in the Whistler, Wilde and Pater period of art for art's sake. You see that's the danger, but the thing *is* worth doing for its own sake and does exist on its own level. It doesn't have to have another purpose.

Not a purpose, but if it exists for its own sake, that means you can write the most marvellous play in the world, stick it in your bottom drawer and it's no good to anybody.

Charles Morgan once wrote about this in one of his plays. Does the thing exist once it's written down or does it only exist with an audience? I should say that it exists anyway.

You can't really tell if it's good until you've seen whether what you've been trying to say can make any impact on an audience.

I don't agree. It's the degree of your talent whether you know, not whether it's good, but whether it's right. I wouldn't say good because this implies a kind of quality which isn't assessable in any art. There's an instinctive feeling of rightness. No, talent isn't a question of putting words on paper – it isn't a question of being clever or anything like that. It's a matter of knowing that what you've done has an essential rightness, and this is the degree of talent I think which is most important. That's why revision is important, because revision can often make something which appears to be pretty ordinary and boring into something most extraordinary.

I know it's a cliché, but there are in any work of art things which the author didn't realise were there.

I quite agree.

Well this is something which the audience have seen in that play. If you say a work of art is worth doing for its own sake, what does that mean? You have a certain vision or a certain insight into something – some episode, some...

But this seems to me to be the very essence of the personal level of our art. I mean there are many things in life on the personal level which are worth doing for their own sake. Making love, for example. They don't need to have repercussions outside themselves, they're intensely personal things.

Why then do you criticise Marching Song *for being too dense? This seems to me to be a criticism of the fact that it doesn't communicate.*

No. I was talking in a literary sense. I was talking more of its style, which no longer satisfies me. I'm not terribly concerned that it doesn't communicate because it's too dense. Frankly I wouldn't take this too far. One would be a lunatic to say that one's aim was to reach a marvellous state of total non-communication. I'm not really saying that, although there are very interesting factors there. If somebody really set out to reach such a state of total non-communication, it would be interesting to see how far the receptivity of an audience does go to see if anyone could get it. I mean if Tennents could put on a play and on the very first night there were the ladies and gentlemen in black ties, the film stars, the agents, the girls, and everybody, and on the second night there was *nobody,* but nobody at all. If you could alienate to that extent – and I very nearly achieved it with *Saint's Day* – it would be very interesting, because you see, time begins to open windows. Totally non-communicated art must be for all time: in other words in twenty years it must still be as utterly and absolutely incomprehensible as if it were put on tomorrow. There is very little art that has ever done this. I don't really preach it and I wouldn't say that's the answer. I'm becoming much more lucid. Now let me tell you something, I'm known as a writer who doesn't communicate easily with the public, but as a person in life I'm reasonably articulate. What's very interesting is that there are a number of playwrights who are apparently communicating beautifully in their plays but as individuals they're totally non-articulate. If you take my attitude that an artist should be non-engaged, then I think that I should be perfectly at liberty to be highly articulate in the play form and absolutely non-articulate on every subject socially or in ordinary prose like a review. But the extraordinary thing about it is that the writers I find inarticulate in life identify themselves much more closely with the necessity to be articulate about things outside plays than I do. They are always charging windmills in a flurry of words. I think I'm more suspicious of life. I'm older, of course. I think, though, I was more suspicious when I was younger.

You could envisage that you might write a play which you thought was the best thing you'd ever done, which was detested by the critics, the public, and everyone whose opinion you respect, and you could still think that this was your masterpiece?

Oh, yes. I have a play not written – but in a very advanced form of planning, which is absolutely impeccable in argument. It's watertight. If the play was written and performed, it would make people so angry – I mean, people would say, 'Surely he's not *so* far right wing? Six years ago we thought him Fascist... *what* are we going to call him now?' And yet, the interesting thing is that there isn't a single argument in the play which isn't absolutely valid. The danger of this thing is this extraordinary sort of sophistry that can come of being too clever. I picked up a copy of a book by de Montherlant the other day, and I've been obsessed for days: it opened in my hand and I found myself staring at a sentence which said, 'He who pities others pities himself.' I merely thought 'Hm!', shut the book and put it down, and went away, but this sentence lodged somewhere. It seems to me a heartbreaking statement by one of the greatest writers in Europe, a genius, I think. I don't know the degree of seriousness in which he wrote it. But this is what I mean by a statement which in our day and age is desperately wrong and yet, it has a *nagging truth.*

Now, the play I have in mind, which I'd like to write, is on this basis. I may do it. If I'm made terribly angry over *The Devils,* I'll probably go away and do it. The danger lies in the introduction of morality, and by morality, I don't mean the social and Christian morality of the middle classes, but the immense new morality which has emanated from the Royal Court. Once you begin to impose this on art, then I think you're in desperate danger. Huxley, I remember, once said that the nearest he had ever been able to define his own position as a writer was as that of a gangster who lives on society, but beyond it, on the edge of it. I think that the Thomas Mann quotation is true, and from the geographical position I think that Huxley is pretty well right. Everyone has become too scrupulous, you see. They all want to be *loved*! They ought to be terrible. And the Press doesn't help. A few years ago it used to be the Russian menace, or something like that, and some quite inoffensive person or movement was blown up to terrify people. But now they choose playwrights. Osborne, for example, has to be a kind of menace – nobody's quite sure what he's menacing. He's terribly interesting and right, but he really hasn't knocked anything down. He has done great things for the theatre, but nothing for society, not really. I think everybody has become much too careful. Then, of course, the commercial pressures are so powerful to deliver the groceries, properly packed, and if possible pre-frozen, so that they will keep.

Does this make Genet one of your favourite authors?

No. Genet is one of my unfavourite authors.

Why do you think that you as a self-confessed disengaged writer have aroused so much enthusiasm and respect from an engaged movement?

I have no idea. I cannot work in this... It's not that I didn't belong to political parties. I did at one time. I'm forty-three tomorrow... I found that I couldn't write within that context. I could not only not write, I couldn't even think. I'm one of that disappearing species, a private individual. As an artist, I mean. They're becoming very rare. I think you must have absolute freedom of action to be able to commit yourself in any contradictory sense. Otherwise I don't see how you can go forward at all.

Do you hold party political convictions of any depth?

I did, before the war. They were very far left, further left than socialism, although I was never a member of the Communist party. Even though I haven't always voted, I've always mentally cast a vote for the Labour party. But over the last year... can't do it.

Would you carry your disengagement so far as to make no distinction between serious and non-serious plays – by non-serious plays, meaning plays written primarily to distract and entertain? Say, Saint's Day *as serious,* A Penny for a Song *as non-serious.*

I don't write to entertain. But... everything's personal, so that everything must be to that extent committed. Obviously, or you don't get anywhere with it. I say I'm not committed. What I really mean is that I'm not committed to any specific movement, because I find it extremely constricting. What some people overlook is that I've never written on any kind of social problem. I've always written on moral problems of a humanist kind, not of a religious kind. *Marching Song,* for example.

Then you probably admire John Arden's work?

Yes, from my own personal point of view, Pinter and Arden are *the* two since the Royal Court started.

Who are, of course, the two who to some extent followed in your footsteps.

Yes, I say 'in a personal sense'.

Would you call Arden an engaged writer?

It's awfully difficult... I don't know how he describes himself... Well, look, the point is this. Arden wrote *Serjeant Musgrave's Dance* with the obvious parallel of Cyprus, but he never underlined the parallel, he just stated it. This is one of the great values of the play, which lifts it from what I've rather loosely called propaganda to a form of art. I also wrote a play, *Marching Song*, about the problems in Europe of an individual – and that's all Arden's play is about. Musgrave and his moral problems – concerning a man who has been put on trial for war crimes. Well, if I'm an engaged writer because of *Marching Song*, so is Arden; but if I'm not, neither is he. The danger with the term 'engagement' is that it becomes understood as propagating the socialist faith, or something like that. I know I occasionally snipe at the Royal Court.

But do you find it exciting?

Of course, of course. This is where I find the naivety of people so extraordinary. Like Wesker, for example, whose actual writings I sometimes admire very much. I think he writes good plays – I never said he didn't. I think he's got the wrong ideas. I think he has highly dangerous ideas. He's like a child wandering around with a bomb. This is the danger nowadays, you see – it can go off, and indeed does go off sometimes. And he'd be the first to be appalled.

The other side of the picture is the blatant right-wing propaganda in seemingly innocuous comedies like Plaintiff in a Pretty Hat. *

There's no doubt about it: the political power of the right wing as opposed to the weakness of the left is partly because

* A West End comedy which opened in October 1956 and ran for 316 performances.

of what has been written. Nothing has been written about the right. The dilemma at the moment, I'm sure, is due to the fact that there's been a lot of extremely uninformed dissemination of half-baked ideas. The power of the Tory party derives from a negative thing. The Labour party, unfortunately, doesn't possess that number of articulate people to actually express its policies. There are an enormous number who are only too prepared at the drop of a hat to rush into print and put down exactly what they think. This has done incalculable harm. The Tory power comes from a lack of expression of their policies. If half-a-dozen people got up and told us what they really thought... How can I put this? Look. Have you ever noticed how eager the Tory press is to print articles by Socialist writers? Now this is not altruism, whatever they may pretend. It's an old trick, allowing a man to talk *himself* into an impossible dilemma. The Tory party has learnt from nineteenth-century politicians that silence is a weapon. It was that silence which revealed the last Labour Party Conference for what it really was. A squalid struggle for power, and nothing to do with a matter of principle. And it's that silence which allows all these mewing little voices to be heard, talking about government in terms of their babies, their aunties and their grandmothers. Christ, when will they learn? And another thing. A brief heresy. Just to end with. Haven't we all been under a misapprehension for too long? Can it be that the masses of the world, in any country, are not really oppressed, but just dumb? In the pejorative sense. Perhaps they don't need to be led, freed, but kicked into action. The history of every revolution proves it. Depressing, isn't it? Let's go back to me.

Finally, Mr Whiting, what do you hope to achieve?

What everyone in my job hopes for, I suppose. A masterpiece.

And how do you propose to set about it?

By becoming more sceptical, and less enthusiastic; by not marching anywhere; by reserving love for women, and not spreading it thinly over the whole of humanity; by not going

THE DEVILS

An Interview with Richard Findlater*
(1961)

I've always been sceptical about the idea that people are influenced by their work, but writing *The Devils* has somehow changed my view of many things. I wrote it with a considerable sense of expectancy – you know that feeling that life and what you write are curiously overlapping, that you put something down on paper and suddenly it *occurs* – and it is much more emotionally charged than my other plays. Working on it has given me a greater awareness of the reality of evil. We talk about love and hate, good and evil, as if they were poles apart, but in fact they're virtually the same thing and in a sense they work in the same way. I no longer believe the old liberal humanist view that man is basically good. He's open to either good or evil. It's up to him which he chooses.

Because *The Devils* is 'about' nuns and priests and their natural traffic with God, it doesn't necessarily mean that it's a religious play. But it's true that I'm a Christian – in the sense that we live in a civilisation which is still shaped by a basically Christian philosophy. I was brought up in the High Church and went to a Low Church school, where the services made me feel bored and rather snobbish: I liked what I'd always had. I still believe in the importance of doctrinal differences between the churches. But I seldom go to a church these days. I'm tired of finding I'm expected to behave as if I'm a member of a boys' club on an outing, instead of worshipping God. I happen to be one of those who aren't in need of that kind of social life. If I do feel lonely or depressed I go to a bar, not to a church...

I read Huxley's *The Devils of Loudun* when it was first published, and I thought at that time that it would make a very good film, though I didn't try to do anything about it.

*After being drama critic of *Time and Tide* from 1960 to 1962, editor of the *Twentieth Century* from 1961-65 and Assistant Editor of the *Observer* from 1963 to 1982, Richard Findlater was appointed as Associate Editor of the *Observer*. His anatomy of the British theatre, *The Unholy Trade*, was published in 1952. He wrote biographies of Emlyn Williams and Michael Redgrave, published in 1956 and 1957.

When Peter Hall approached me two years ago and asked me to write a play for him, I suggested this as one of two subjects: the other was Rolfe's *Hadrian the Seventh*. It had to be a costume play. Peter intended this – whatever it was – to be the first new play in his Aldwych venture, and he felt that a modern-dress drama would have been too great a break with the rest of the repertoire. I knew the type of stage he was planning to use, and I had the opportunity of seeing it in action at Stratford before I began to write the play. But I didn't write with any particular actor or actress in mind, though I knew that Dorothy Tutin might be in the play and that she would be ideal for Sister Jeanne, if I could pull it off.

I planned the play for over a year before I started to write it, making notes and sketches. I began it last March, and then I wrote it far more quickly than I've ever written a play before. Partly, I think, because I worry less these days. Partly because I *had* to finish it. It's hard for me to finish a play unless I'm contractually bound: it's the business of committing oneself to a final text. And I believe that nowadays I'm more practised in getting to the point. Working in films has helped me, from a technical point of view. Anyway, I wrote the first draft in four months instead of taking about two years to do it. There was one interruption, when I got stuck in the second act. I decided to take a rest from it for a few days, so I put my car on an aeroplane to France. I didn't have any idea of going to Loudun originally, but I found myself driving there. It was a very curious experience to see the town, after living in it for so long in my imagination. I hadn't done much research, as I didn't want to be bogged down by fact when I was writing the play. I suppose it must have released me in some way – I don't know – and I came back and finished the whole play. On July 19.

Censorship? It's true that the Lord Chamberlain's office asked me to make cuts and alterations, and with Peter Wood I had to see Colonel Penn – who's been attacked over *Fings Ain't Wot They Used T'Be*. But none of the cuts and alterations have really damaged the play. Where I was forced to rewrite passages, I think I improved the play in a theatrical and literary sense: it wasn't all loss. And although I had to cut out a whole speech by Sister Jeanne in the second act, I shan't print it when I publish the play – though I shall probably put back the other cuts. I must in all honesty say that I have a great respect for the Lord Chamberlain's office. They made it perfectly clear what they wanted, in letters and meetings, and were always open to discussion. I think the Lord Chamberlain has been very generous, in regard to what he has *not* cut. I don't believe that we ought to have a censor; but while we *do* have one, the Lord Chamberlain's men do the job very well.

I could have written *The Devils* with one set and five characters and put it on at a small theatre, but it wouldn't necessarily have been a smaller play. What I find so fascinating about the theatre is that it has such enormous range; and – quite apart from my personal feelings about *The Devils* – I hope that it shows you can commission plays on this scale, as a matter of policy. I've been immensely lucky. I was given everything I wanted. No compromise whatsoever was made, and there is an enormously high standard of production and design. How many English playwrights in the last 300 years, after all, have been given the kind of opportunity that Peter Hall gave me? But other people can do the same: there are many more playwrights than you might imagine who could write a large-scale narrative play if somebody offered them a stage and a company. Fashion has swung too far towards the unplotted, unmotivated play – it's restricting the size of the drama.

ABOUT THE THEATRE

WRITING FOR ACTORS

(1952)

The art of writing for actors has fallen into disrepute. The idea that plays are written bearing in mind that they are to be performed appears to disturb many people nowadays. It is easy to understand how this state of affairs has come about. No form lends itself more easily to the meretricious and the cheap than the theatre. No other art can provide such immediate and extensive, although ephemeral, gratification to the practitioners. There have been those – and their names often rank very high in theatrical history – who have used the theatre and the credulity of large crowds to practise what, in the end, proved to be nothing more than the tricks practised by the experienced on the innocent. A conjurer at a children's party does much the same.

Throughout the history of the theatre this kind of magic can be found. The most guilty men were usually actors; often they were what are called 'great actors'. They achieved much of this sleight-of-hand by the commission of dramatic works to their own dictation or by the mutilation and perversion of existing plays. In this way many great moments of theatre were achieved, but the play went limping off to take refuge between the covers of a book. The excuse for these virtuoso players is not difficult to find. Authors have, during the past hundred and fifty years, provided actors with everything to act except plays. They were given for performance epic poems, political and sociological pamphlets, religious tracts, novels and newspaper reports. Because of this the best actors, who are animals with a strong sense of self-preservation and considerable ingenuity, put together, usually without benefit of so commonplace an object as a book of words, a number of well-dressed and surprising situations which found considerable favour with the innocent. This was very poor art but extremely good business.

We live in a less credulous and, theatrically, more scrupulous age. The measure of a great actor is no longer what he can achieve in prescribed circumstances but what he can achieve with the full weight of the author's intention. There remains, however, much doubt even today. Is the rabbit from the hat alive or is it stuffed? Influenced by this, it is natural that any play of today which *seems* to have been primarily written for actors should be regarded with suspicion. (It is not only natural, it is right: every work of art should be approached with extreme suspicion.) Natural, also, that it should be carefully examined to see that it is not merely an excuse for virtuosity – for fine voices, beautiful clothes and settings and a dazzling, ingenious lighting plot. It must always be remembered that workers in the theatre possess enough technical trickery to deceive even the very discerning. It must also be remembered that never before has it been so scrupulously used. On this basis it is interesting to examine the relation between the dramatic author – who is not, contrary to general opinion, a technical trick – and his actors.

The actor's art provides the dramatist with an instrument of great range. So great, indeed, that only a fool would attempt to employ it without due consideration and seriousness. For the actor's power lies not in his voice, his face or his mind, but in his humanity. Only in the theatre can we call upon men as men to interpret and communicate. That communication can be achieved with great sympathy by an actor lacking, as it does, the bonds of academicism. It is strange the actor's art should be deplored because of its transience. Surely the emotional, the moving quality of the actor's performance is that it is gone into the past as irrevocably as any human action, that it possesses a mortality of its own.

The actor's concern is to achieve, not a truth, but a rightness. There is no constant in human behaviour and it is with human behaviour the actor deals.

To perfect this rightness is the job of the actor. Clothes, make-up, movement, even the words of the part are subsidiary equipment. From whatever point the actor may approach a part, however much he may change his appearance, the part he plays will have firm foundation in the actor's personality as a man. Once he has identified the character of the part with his own personality the words, moves and idiosyncrasies fall naturally into place. There is no necessity to memorise them in the usual sense of the word – a common misconception – for after a period of rehearsal there is no conscious effort to remember what is said or done and when. Such things come from the rightness of the performance.

The degree of greatness in a performance depends on the power of identification which springs in sympathy from the individual personality of the player. This plans an ideal performance in the mind which, in fact, may never be given either in rehearsal or before an audience; yet, from this ideal can be taken the performance for the theatre. Delacroix expresses this vividly: 'He (the actor) makes tracings, so to speak, of the original idea.' The similarity and detail of these tracings will determine the fineness of subsequent performances.

An actor will expect from a new play not that it should be merely a book of words containing a narrative in dramatic form, but that it should provide a stimulus to his imagination. It is at this point that the author and his actors first come together.

What else must the author have prepared to bring about this fusion? From the director's and actor's points of view he must have prepared a blueprint, a coldly technical document. This may suggest the subordination of the writer in the theatre as a creator. There is an old argument as to whether the direction and performance of a play is interpretative or creative. The question can be answered: the writing, directing, designing and acting of a play are each creative in their own part to the whole. More important, surely, is that they are interdependent. It is an author's vanity to claim creation because he is the mere starting point. His play would be no play if it remained words on paper.

The modern play is not a work of literature. Unfortunately, it is often considered and criticised as such not only from the printed page but from performance. It is not unusual to find critics who are capable of translating words spoken by an actor back into the written word, and on that written word they make their judgement. This is understandable. Performances in a theatre are difficult to judge dispassionately – at least, they should be difficult to judge – and the printed word has stability. Nevertheless, it is a mistake to judge plays in such a way. Acquaintance with the text is admirable, though rare, but criticism should be confined to performance.

The concern, therefore, is not with 'good prose' or with 'good verse' in the accepted sense. The structure is action and the action is controlled and formed by dialogue. The action must never become subordinated to the dialogue. In the modern play, which is attempting to achieve a greater unity of time and place, much difficulty can be experienced in carrying forward narrative. More difficulty, for example, than would be experienced in a play of such structure by the Elizabethan dramatists, who were not generally attempting unity of time or place. This allows for a considerable complexity of plot, as in certain plays by Shakespeare. It would be impossible and not in the least desirable to attempt such goings-on in a modern two or three act play. It has been attempted in recent years in historical plays usually with lamentable results.

The shaping of prose dialogue determines the style. This does not mean the characteristic idiom of the dialogue but the use of voices to achieve dramatic form. Not what is said or how it is said but *when*. For example, the exact placing of unbroken passages for a single voice or dialogue in half-speeches for two or more voices perhaps speaking together. By this method it is possible to control from within the text of the play the speed and exact rhythm which are usually imposed by the director. Also, in this form, the play can be 'read' from the printed page without regard to theme, or in this case sense, in very much the same way as a musical score.

The actor can then see the dramatic shape of an individual part within a scene and not be forced to rely on an intuitive sense which is sometimes false and leads to distortion.

The basic, the unalterable factor of drama is the moment 'when'; the moment of happening which is contained in the action. The dramatist must concern himself with this moment of action and not leave it, as so often happens, to be imposed by the director or players. In other words, the dramatist must create what is done and *when,* and not only the words to be spoken. During the past years much critical enquiry has taken place to determine a style of playwriting. Almost without exception this enquiry has dealt with the form of the spoken word. Yet this is not the starting point. There is no unhappier sight in the world than an actor at rehearsal searching for the motive of the words he is given to speak. There is an old and, alas, only half-humorous dictum of the theatre: never pay any attention to the author's stage directions. Those directions, however, are the author's first means of communication with his actors. They must never be mechanical directions – where to move, how to sit. Nor must they presume to instruct – to be said 'angrily', 'sadly', 'bitterly'. They must augment the words to be spoken. They are a guideline of motive and action throughout the individual parts and, when translated into action in performance, as much part of the play as the spoken word.

All this is a plea for a greater discipline and exactness in the transcription for action. Perhaps it will be wise to work towards a script which is only comprehensible to the theatre worker and remains nonsense to the layman. It is interesting to speculate on the harm done to the play in the theatre by the fact that it is expected the text should be readable by the non-expert. Other forms – the film, television, radio – have begun to devise a method of transcription for their actors which is far from readable in any pleasurable sense yet admirably suits the demands for translation into performance. The theatre, however, remains tied to an outmoded convention. Every other factor in the theatre – playing, designing, staging, lighting – has developed with the age. The text of the play alone remains unchanged, an archaism.

In rehearsal the author's contact with the actors is through the director of the play. In this relation there must be, of course, considerable sympathy and respect. From the moment a play is in the hands of a director, the technical resources for translation to performance are brought into action. At this point it is often considered that the author's job is finished. Very often at this time the author hides himself. He should not do this. The author is as much a worker *in* the theatre as directors, designers, actors and the rest. He cannot deliver a play and then sit back with no further participation. At the stage of the first rehearsal his work is not half done. The position of an author at rehearsals is certainly not an enviable one. It calls for a high degree of tact and great consideration of actors' problems, for it is here the play becomes a work of collaboration and, as in all works of collaboration, there must necessarily be considerable adjustment. A slavish and literal representation of the printed play by the director and actors is as wrong as misrepresentation for the sake of virtuosity. These problems arise because the direction and acting of a play in the modern idiom is, in detail, a thing of inspiration and improvisation in the moment of rehearsal. Only the very broad and, of necessity, practical details of production can be laid down before rehearsal. The creation of the play, the intangible substances, the magic, the poetry and mood are drawn from the text sometimes by so prosaic a method as trial and error during rehearsal. Indeed, rehearsals are not the time spent to get everything right but to get everything wrong. Such methods can prove most difficult for an author. There is the constant necessity for adjustment in detail while the structure and essence of the play must be retained. It is vital that the limits of this adjustment should be previously laid down between the author and director; limits not only within the play as a whole but within its units, the individual characters and scenes. An example of this adjustment is that an actor may, by imagination in his performance, make certain words unnecessary. The emotional content of a scene may crowd out the necessity for the spoken word. The lines, therefore, are well deleted. There should be no deletion, however, without replacement by another factor – emotional or visual, perhaps – otherwise the overall structure of the play is affected.

This formal structure is the poetry of drama. Given this, anything is possible to the actor. From it he can build in a disciplined and poetic way. Without it he will retreat into naturalism, and instead of acting he will behave.

The theatre in this day has an opportunity to become an art in its own right. In the past twenty-five years much dead wood from theatrical convention has been taken over by the cinema. In the same way television is going to relieve the cinema of many elements it can well do without, leaving it a freer and purer form.

A time has been reached when the terms of theatre and of dramatic art generally need to be redefined. Dramatists of today suffer from a set of values derived from every artistic form under the sun. The body of the theatre is immensely, wonderfully healthy; the mind wanders a little at the moment but only from indecision, not from a permanent derangement. If the value of the theatre as an independent art can be assessed, and that art practised by writers, it may be possible to talk about the modern play in the same sense as modern music and modern painting.

A CONVERSATION

(1953)

B: You begin.

A: *If I do you must promise not to trap me into damaging admissions. I hate a fuss – yet I like being self-contradictory. It's boring to stick to the point, don't you think?*

B: I promise not to let you make a fool of yourself, if that's what you mean.

A: *I didn't mean that.* (There is a long silence.) *Well?*

B: May I quote something?

A: *From that book you're holding? If it will give you pleasure.*

B: 'A play does not interest me unless the external action, simplified as much as possible, is only a pretext for the exploration of man; unless the author has undertaken, not to imagine and put together a mechanical plot, but to express activities of the human soul with the greatest truthfulness, intensity and depth.'

A: *May I remind you that we're in England. It's most unfair to quote a French dramatist in that way. I say again – we are in England.*

B: Where do you stand?

A: *Under cover. To be a dramatist in this country today is to be placed on the lunatic fringe of Showbiz. It is apt that T C Worsley* should have called his collected dramatic criticisms* The Fugitive Art, *for not only is it eluding the practitioners at the moment but it is also in active flight.*

B: From what?

A: *Being put on ice in more senses than one.*

B: What are we talking about?

A: *Your grandfather and the vicar's sister used to call it The Drama.*

B: I know what you mean.

A: *It's being carried along on the floodtide of the Entertainment Industry. It has almost lost the position of an art in its own right.*

*Drama critic of the *New Statesman*.

Unless it is re-established – and that damned quickly – it will die as the music-hall and the circus have died. They were individual arts which in an attempt to remain popular absorbed the worst elements of other mediums and therefore lost their personality. The theatre is in that danger at the moment.

B: Can anything be done?

A: *Don't look so anxious. Some people believe the answer to be an alliance with literature, which they hold to be the parent of the theatre. I can't see this myself. In the past the partnership between literature and the theatre in this country has always been uneasy. Times have not changed since Byron wrote, 'Since such an attempt to drag me forth as a gladiator in the theatrical arena is a violation of all the courtesies of literature, I trust that the impartial part of the press will step between me and this pollution.' Strong words to use when objecting to a production. Again, one of the most tragic histories in literature is the five years spent by Henry James sincerely and devotedly writing for the theatre and ending with the heartcry, 'I may have been meant for the Drama – God knows! – but I certainly wasn't meant for the Theatre.' Read his plays and you will understand why. They are dramatically impossible.*

B: Surely a play can be written for the solitary reader and need not come into actual performance. That, I should have thought, is the true literary play.

A: *Exactly. And it demonstrates the whole failure of the purely literary play in the theatre. Of course the theatre would benefit from more plays by English writers prominent in other fields such as the novel. Nobody denies that. But the writers must meet the theatre half-way. The play has a technique of its own – a very obvious thing to say but it's remarkable how few writers understand that and believe they can use it as a kind of hobby-horse. Naturally, it throws them off. There are problems beyond the use of language. I don't mean problems of staging, either. That sort of thing can be left in the hands of the director and designer. The problems are mainly concerned with writing for actors. It is odd that with all the talk about a literary theatre the highest points in dramatic literature should have been reached by men who were actors or men who had a great and intimate knowledge of the theatre as a place.*

B: You mentioned the failure of the purely literary play in the theatre. Surely –

A: *I'm going to interrupt you. Do you mind? At the moment there are two plays running in London which are of great interest in this connection. The first is Terence Rattigan's* The Deep Blue Sea. *The language in this play is intentionally almost entirely dependent on very worn everyday speech. There are times, indeed, when whole passages of the play could go unheard and the attention of an audience would remain because the story and atmosphere at these points are carried forward by other means. By the way, there are moments of suspended action in this production which are the most courageous and effective thing of their kind I've ever seen. But to get on – the second play is* The Living Room, *by Graham Greene. As you know, this is a first play by a distinguished novelist. Here the characters are startlingly unoriginal. We have seen them all before in other circumstances. Every one of them is a theatrical cliché – the maladjusted psychologist, the calm, legless, frustrated priest in a wheelchair, the two mad old women and the young girl who's sexually passionate but fundamentally innocent. The dialogue in* The Living Room *is again entirely flat. It's not even characteristic as it is in Rattigan's play. Both plays start with these apparent disadvantages and yet – this is the point – both yield everything to be asked of a performance in a theatre. 'Words, words, words!' lamented a critic some time ago. 'However imaginative or inventive the actor or producer, it comes back in the end to words.' But it doesn't, and these two plays prove it. Greene has upset many of the critics by writing a play as a dramatist and not as a novelist.*

B: Are you suggesting that both these plays owe their excellence to direction and performance?

A: *No, I'm not. The direction of both plays is masterly and the performances without exception are first-rate. But there is a form, a manner, in both plays which comes from the author as creator and not from the executants. It is this manner which makes them exciting and satisfying. If I was very old-fashioned I might refer you to something called 'theatre', but I can no longer do that in this analytical age without being laughed at as a sentimentalist. There is no magic left in art nowadays. Anyone can be taught the tricks of the trade. It's as inhuman as war. In a theatre the auditorium is enemy territory. The dramatist can only draw up the plans for the campaign which are put into operation by his Chief of Staff, the director, and then leave the actors to fight the battle nightly.*

B: I suppose we'd better talk about the dilemma of the young dramatist.

A: *I suppose so. Everybody does.*

B: Why are there so few plays?

A: *You sound like a headline. It's not a question of quantity. At the moment there are hundreds of plays being written in this country. But to judge from the past few years only a few will be any good. You're going to ask me why so many will be bad? Because there have always been bad plays and there always will be. What do those professional mourners, the critics, want? I remember reading in a newspaper recently that in a given period of time – I think it was ten months – there had only been six plays produced in the West End of London which had been worth seeing. I think six is a considerable number. After all, how many symphonies receive their first performance each year? This country is more fortunate than it will admit in its dramatists. It has at least four who are regularly writing plays of importance. Mind you, the confusion of most dramatic critics – that job which is only a little better than an underground railway porter – is understandable when you remember that they have to see everything. That's a penalty of Showbiz. Other critics are more fortunate.* The Times *music critic is not asked to cover everything from Bayreuth to Johnny Ray.*

B: It is believed in some quarters –

A: *Speak up.*

B: I say, some people believe that there are many good plays which are never produced. First plays by unknown authors.

A: *Of course they believe that. There are so many bad plays staged that the natural muddle-headed conclusion is that there must be a compensating number of good plays which are never seen. This is a very English way of looking at things – the no-nonsense way –*

playwriting and coalmining – the stuff's down there so go and dig it out. By the way, this notion that there are hundreds of unplayed masterpieces around recently led to a suggestion which is superb in its lunacy. There were some letters in a responsible paper advising the completely joyless idea that every play written should first be produced by amateur theatres. The main advocate for this, if I remember rightly, was a gentleman living in Aldershot. West End managers would then be invited to view these productions and from them select plays for London. If there was one grain of sense in this suggestion – and there is not – the attitude alone shows an unbearable sign of defeat and timidity. It is saying in effect, 'Let's fight the battle and see if it can be won, and if it can't be, then don't let's fight it.' I only mention this to demonstrate to what depths of silliness the apparently interminable argument over the 'lost plays' can descend.

B: But a new play written in English will be produced if it's any good. Do you really believe that?

A: *Of course. Good plays are too rare to ignore. It's a myth that there are hundreds of masterworks which nobody will buy. Managers aren't fools. I should have thought that since the war, when almost every worthwhile play which has been seen in London has been presented by what are called commercial managements, that old dragon would have died a natural death. Yet the idea continues to be fostered that neither managers, directors nor actors (they say actors are notoriously bad judges!) are capable of appreciating a play in script form. Who is capable, then? The gentleman from Aldershot, presumably. Seriously, you can have no complaint about a management which produces, say, a Sartre play and the Gielgud season at one end of the scale and Wilfred Pickles* at the other end. That is not a scale of excellence or importance, either. It just depends on the type of play you're intending to write. You are intending to write a play, aren't you?*

B: (*bursting into tears*) Yes.

A: *Come, now. You're not obliged to write it, are you?*

B: No, I'm not. I hadn't thought of that.

A: *Nobody does, it seems.*

*A comedian popular on the radio.

B: Listen to me! No, let me speak! I'm sure that very soon the theatre will break through to something new and exciting. A play will suddenly be there. One evening – one ordinary winter evening – that terrible first-night audience will go into a theatre expecting the usual 'show'. The curtain will go up and the first words will be spoken – and then! – everyone in that theatre will know that they're seeing something which is going to have an effect throughout the rest of history.

A: *I say!*

B: That's my vision. That's what I dream about when it doesn't keep me awake at night.

A: *Has it ever occurred to you that the play form may have reached the ultimate point of development a long time ago? The form seems to have stuck fast – gone aground somewhere, doesn't it? I mean, if you're content to take an earlier form and write your plays within that considered shape – say, as used by Ibsen or, if you'd rather, Pinero – then you'll probably write very excellent and successful plays. If, however, you have ideas of developing form and inventing a new type of structure, then I think it's better to use plasticine. When I say the ultimate point of development, I'm thinking really of the way in which the dramatic form has contracted. Take the physical limitations alone: the absurd size of the proscenium, the narrow lines of sight, the irritating convention of intervals for food and drink and going to the lavatory and the curse of an exact length in time to within ten minutes. We have to accept all these limitations, and the scholars tell us that the imposition of limits make for better art, but I can't bring myself to believe that a man works best shut up in a box. The logical conclusion would seem to be the building of a fourth wall in brick. The films are very excited by the discovery of a third dimension. The way of development for the play is probably something of the kind, but not in a physical sense, for a lion in your lap isn't as stimulating as an idea in your head. I believe that there's a further dimension to the play and a dimension that can be used in a drawing-room set cluttered up with furniture and all the limitations we've mentioned. I'm not suggesting that there's anything new about it. Only a progression to break through to a further reality than is immediately*

apparent from the physical aspect. Let me put it this way. It has become very fashionable to have a stage setting designed with a transparent wall. By this means it has become possible to show action taking place beyond the point you would normally expect. The problem of the transparent wall belongs to the director and the designer, but the problem of the use of transparency in the characters of a play belongs to the dramatist. Read that quotation from de Montherlant again. No, don't bother. It's a matter of behaviour. We have become used to assessing the behaviour of characters on the stage in very much the same way as we assess people in social life. The play, however, doesn't demand the complex and artificial standards of everyday life. What Michel Saint Denis* has called 'the mud of naturalism' has so plastered the characters of modern plays that it's no longer possible to see the man beneath. Now many of us are no longer attempting to portray the man but only the mud-man. If you hear the cry go up in a theatre, 'People don't do such things!' look closer. It may be rewarding. The exact reproduction of human social behaviour is mere journalism. It has nothing to do with writing plays.
(There is a second long silence.)

B: I must be off now.

A: *Must you? Well, thank you for giving me an opportunity to discuss all this. It's something I rarely do, and I've found it a delightful experience. We must meet again and next time you must let me do the talking. Goodbye.*

B: Goodbye.

---

*A French director who settled in London and ran the Old Vic Theatre School from 1946 to 1952 and directed several productions at the Old Vic, including *Oedipus Rex* with Laurence Olivier in 1945.

THE PURPOSE OF THEATRE

(Undated)

The purpose of the theatre, as of any art, is to give an awareness of the human condition. It must, therefore, be religious in intention, for an understanding of man's state comes by acceptance of God. A great performance in the theatre, a great performance of music, is a religious experience if only by the delegation of creative power to man. Equally, all performances are ritualistic in that they are rehearsed, as near predestined as man can make them. The work of creation in art by man is an attempt to come to terms with order, and to bring that ordered experience within the awareness of others.

It is not a question of argument or conviction now. Today, a playwright does not ask that an audience should go from the theatre with the words, 'I accept' or 'I do not accept'. He asks that they say, simply, 'I understand'. It is their own reasoning which must then take them either to solitary contemplation or to the barricades.

The responsibility of the poet and playwright is very great today. Language has become perverted. The most beautiful and meaningful words have become cheapened. And it is by words we understand. If the purity of expression is fouled, language becomes a lunatic chatter, the sound of apes. Behaviour follows. The writer must resist by speaking in his own true voice. Then the language will be real and unsoiled, and the man will not be a puppet. That is the great responsibility of the artist today. To stand against being used.

Every man goes under the illusion that his dilemma is unique, that he is the victim of particular injustice. Art shows the dilemma to be universal. The state of the tragic hero is the state of all men. To struggle and to die. The suppression of this truth by promises of happiness, comfort, ease and insensibility is the greatest crime against mankind, for there can be no tyranny when the truth is relentlessly exposed. Yet man forges his own chains by his fear of truth. It is the artist's absolute right to break the bonds of silence and conspiracy. The theatre gives that opportunity.

When the day comes and there are no great theatres, we shall fall in the dark. That time is not yet, thank God.

FROM A NOTEBOOK (1)

(1956)

'The essence of drama is in the dilemma of the central heroic figure.' Caught somewhere on the curve of rise, triumph, fall. Hamlet, exquisitely planning his own destruction: Sid Field setting out to learn to play golf. Same thing. The crumbling of confidence, the rise of injustice, the death of trust, the disintegration of man. Both moving. Both theatre.

❖

The most dangerous tendency of modern criticism towards the work of young writers, especially in the theatre, is that it sets out to destroy by ridicule or abuse the writer's private mythology. Yet it is this private world which prevents the play becoming mere bombast, or journalism. If we are normal human beings we live surrounded by terrors, clowns, dead loves and old fears, represented by, say, a painting on a wall, some reels of photographic negative, a rose garden and a call from another room. The artist, admitting their significance, naturally reaches out for them in the desperate emergency of creation. They are nothing in themselves, these material things, but what they evoke for us as writers matters very much. Certainly if we fail to communicate this to an audience it demonstrates our failure as artists. But the fact that we use them does not demonstrate our failure as men, as is so often implied. What is often mistaken for symbolism nowadays is no more than the bare bones of the art we are practising. In the theatre we are dealing with people at a certain place, at a certain time. Everything, therefore, as in life, must take on a certain significance as a symbol. Told that we are writing fantasy we can only answer that it is an accurate recreation of reality. The sensible man, seeing through his own lunatic eyes, denies it. It is the dilemma of all modern art.

❖

John Gielgud at rehearsal, speaking to a nervous actor:

'Tread the stage as if it were a battlefield – ' and then adding, aside, 'which, my God, it is.'

❖

The theatre seems to want to be the place where everything is neatly tidied up. Compensation. Here we can see how it all ends, find out who finishes up in the marriage bed, and who in the coffin. It is a place where people actually communicate with each other, sensibly, and where there is an orderliness, the lack of which drives us mad in everyday life. That's why when something goes wrong in performance, an actor forgets his words or misses an entrance, it seems to be the grossest breach of good manners. The audience look aside, appalled, and there is some hysteria. So we have a passion for the well-made play, the well-graced actor. They don't let us down. Their pauses are of exactly the right length, not so long that we see beyond to reality. Hohum! I suppose this is art.

❖

Critics always review as if the play had been written for them. Nonsense! Everything is written for some girl or other. And who ever loved a critic?

❖

Saint's Day. That play has the roots of anything I can do in the theatre. Perhaps every man's first play has that. I came very near to putting on paper the exact play, the blueprint for actors. It was entirely the concern of the theatre. In the true sense, an experiment. That was the real argument of the time (forgotten now) between people of the theatre and critics (the audience never became involved as far as I could see). Actors found in the play, as the actual players did, a disciplined form of notation, which yet allowed for flexible interpretation. The content? A different matter, certainly. I was right, though, to put it down as I did: I was wrong not to develop it in another play. It laid the way for the

London production of such plays as *Waiting for Godot,* not in a literary sense because it's not comparable, but as a technique. They were both written in the same year.

❖

Marching Song. It has all the classical virtues of a thoroughbred play. Yet for me it remains bleak and white. Unlike *Saint's Day* it has no private parts.

❖

This business of the play's first performance in London. The 'first night'. My own experience. Getting up late. Looking in the paper to make sure it's the right day. Around noon sending telegrams to the actors. Lunch, with a friend. Carefully chosen. Preferably someone I've known long, and who will not expect conversation. A pretty actress, not of the cast, does very nicely. The ideal would probably be someone newly met, and to fall in love over the meal table. This has never been possible. In the afternoon, a film. An American musical or Western seems right. Anything remotely connected with the subject of the play, or written by an admired writer, must be avoided. (Henry James spent the first night of *Guy Domville* watching *An Ideal Husband.* This is really perverse.) Some tea, alone. This provides the one moment of the day for introspection, and gives an opportunity for any tears to be shed. Then somewhere to dress, playing heroic music on a gramophone, and drinking enough, but not too much, whisky. A taxi to the theatre, through London at its sweetest time: after the rush, a little before dark (all plays should open in the spring or late summer). At the theatre, looking up to understand the dreadful inadequacy of the title. Going down the alley, past the garbage bins, to the stage door. Deform my clothes with a bundle of telegrams. See the actors. Never fail to be touched by their great kindness, at such a time of nervousness and tension. Then to the auditorium. Friends: their behaviour is the same as at the maternity hospital. Enemies: their behaviour is the same as at the law courts. See well-known people who don't know me. Sit down, trapped in the middle of the fifth row.

I've never yet had a theatre with a centre aisle. The curtain goes up, and the audience starts coming in. I sit like a dummy. An interval. In the rush for the bars I seem to be left alone in the stalls. I can't go to the bar, and I can't hang about the corridors where even the most defiant smile will appear ingratiating. I sit, until the end. There seems to be no applause. Backstage, the actors greet me as if I've been away for years. I love every one of them. I find myself at a supper party. It seems everyone is out of their wits about the play. There is a man who had a word with Shulman, and at least he didn't speak against the play. I have had no coherent word with anyone. So I go home. The London streets have a few people in them who don't care. I read the telegrams and fall asleep wondering who sent best wishes from all at Chipping Campden.

Ah! what novelists miss.

❖

An uneasy truce seems always to exist in Western Europe between literature and the theatre. When sniping occurs it is always one-sided. The remarks of Byron, George Moore, Henry James and Gide against the theatre have sometimes been very sour. They were rarely answered. There is something very funny in such men, as seen from their letters and journals, often holding a deep liking for the theatre as a member of the audience, coming down into the market-place, their trousers up to their knees, to work for it. Yeats is the wonderful example to the contrary. But then he was working at a time of crisis, which is a time for the theatre. The revolutionary theatre in Russia, Germany in the 1920s, the Abbey Theatre, France in the 1940s. And London at that time. There was an opportunity then for the writing of plays. It was missed. There was an audience we've never had since. No one found it worth their while to write with any seriousness for it. Classical revivals and farce. It thrived on them.

❖

I am getting old. I found myself the other day wishing that there could be a play unexpectedly performed in London, brilliant, successful, the critics enraptured, and written by someone about twenty years old. Is this too much to hope for nowadays? Or is the theatre getting old? Such things are in the past. As a critic said to me the other day when speaking of my plays, 'Cheer up, nobody writes anything much – especially for the theatre – until they're past forty.' Consolation? No.

❖

The theatre in the provinces is dwindling fast. Appeals are made, committees formed, a temporary prop is found. It fails. There is another furniture store or ice rink. None of this should really be surprising. I recently saw a performance in a theatre a little way from London. The entrance and auditorium were lit by small yellow dusty lights. The rogue's gallery of actors' photographs ogled me, hung against peeling wallpaper, crooked. The bar was tiled like a public lavatory. The performance, which lasted something over three hours, was of a play which everyone could understand, but no one could have cared about. In the intervals a curtain was lowered advertising corsets and Tudor Tea Rooms, while an elderly man played Delibes, Gilbert and Sullivan and Edward German on a muffled piano in the pit. An audience of about fifty people were huddled in coats against the cold. One of them, speaking of the pianist, said, 'Very good, this fellow, Keeps away from all this modern trash.' It seemed the final word for the whole place.

❖

There is something very mysterious about the amateur theatre in this country. Why do they do it? And in such numbers. This behaviour, this public performing, does not square with the accepted view of our national characteristics. We are a nation of secret actors, there's no getting away from it. In university cities professional theatres wither and die, yet every college has a group of young men dressed in sheets declaiming hours of Fletcher or Dekker or Ford, which must have taken them weeks to memorise. It's all very strange.

❖

The tall figure, remote, young, the black velvet falling from shoulder to foot, caught from my viewpoint most upright against the curve of an arch. The turn of that astonishing head, which, though bare, seemed banded with iron. The superb resignation, yet decision, in the lines, 'Not a whit, we defy Augury; there's a special Providence in the fall of a sparrow'. Paul Scofield as Hamlet. I've never before seen this moment of the play held as it should be with such effect to accentuate the fall to the final action. He is a great actor.

❖

I have yet to write a play which gives no offence on the grounds of bad taste. In each one, in the original version, a line or situation has been pointed out to me. Humiliated, I have removed it. So we all become trimmers, tacking cleverly before the supposedly scented breath of popular taste. When there is a fight about something, such as *Waiting for Godot,* it is fought with pillows and no gaiety. Why don't playwrights criticise each other? Everybody is on everybody else's side, presenting a solid front to absolutely nothing. The theatre represents itself as a deserving charity. The hat is always being handed round. It has been dying for years. At first the public waited beside the bed, but now, yawning, it has gone away. The confidence trick has failed. The invalid must get out of its bed, and get on with its job. But, like a hopeless hypochondriac, alienating even the affections of the most fond, it cannot stop talking about its ailments. They are, naturally, of the most socially acceptable kind. Genteel poverty brought about by taxation, lack of support from its near relative, literature, and no good home. Yet everybody writes plays, or so it seems. Schoolmasters, critics, clergymen, factory hands rush to it as a form. Sixteen are on my table at the moment. Every one within the first few pages states, I was written for so-and-so to act, or I was written after seeing the last Eliot play, or I was written because my author, a man of great integrity, needs money and thinks football pools vulgar. Not one says, I was written because the girl's gone off and I'm so bloody miserable at not having anybody in my bed any more and I can't stand looking at the night sky all night so I've put a shilling the last in the meter and I'm writing down how good she was tasted good she did and now she's gone so here's the story of yours truly in three acts. People should appreciate the pleasure of writing in obscurity. Don't they know the first public notice of the first public performance finishes you? From then on the game is politics. It has to be. You've got to get on. You've got to make a living. You've got to consider the sensibilities of others. You're not writing for your wastepaper basket. You're writing for a public. And critics. And managers. And posterity. You hope. So, with an eye cocked at all these you think, What shall I write? And there is a long, long pause.

❖

I suppose nothing is going to make me angry or sad enough to write a new play. Sitting in the weak sunshine it seems as unimportant to me as it would seem to anyone else. Perhaps it really is the climate. In a little over a year I shall be forty. All the people who urged me to write for the theatre ten years ago have husbands and children now, and are not concerned with anger or sadness. I am becoming petulant, but it has no irritant value, except to others.

❖

A way of salvation: make enemies.

THE WRITERS' THEATRE

(1956)

There is sometimes talk of a Writers' Theatre. This, I take it, means a theatre where the dramatist is pre-eminent, where all other functions such as director, designer and actors are interpreters of the supreme text. At first sight, this must seem to be the one possible working foundation for the theatre as an art. The play, as music, is written as a personal act, the work of a man, and is interpreted in public performance. Yet this is not the case, if we are to judge from the arguments put forward for a theatre on such a basis. Even now, in England, we rarely argue for the establishment of something already existing. So it must be accepted that the English theatre is not a writers' theatre.

The question, Is it possible to make a play in performance a work of art? has troubled writers from the beginning of what must be called the modern theatre. That is, performances in a playhouse under the stringent conditions of time and place which have been dictated by the caprice and fashion of the audience. It is this condition, more than any other, which gives to playwriting an air of servility. Also the fact that actors have a strange love for humiliation. It was, I believe, David Garrick who first used the phrase 'servants of the public' in reference to actors. It was a mistake. From that moment the mob was at the throat, and has never let go. Now it is shaking the life from the theatre, and still the words are, We exist by your favour.

Nonsense. No art exists by any man's favour. Public entertainment certainly does so, but an art exists in its own right as something worth doing for its own sake. A play, like any other created work, must have the arrogance of its convictions.

As a literary form the play is very unsatisfactory. The performance of a play cannot be arrived at without a hundred compromises on the part of the writer. This would seem to make it a worthless pursuit. But there remains the intention.

It is this. Some twenty-five thousand words form a pattern of *present* action – in which the play differs from any other literary form – and in this way must present a problem of such urgency that it cannot be dealt with retrospectively. The thing must happen before the eyes. It must be witnessed. That is the intention of a play.

It is this intention which has kept the form alive. And kept going the struggle to bring about a successful transition from the printed page to the stage.

The text contains a pattern of action based on time and place. It contains the spoken word which should rigidly control the physical action. By this I mean that all action should spring from the word spoken. This action must, being of the present, be forward moving in time within any one scene. The language of the play, which will determine the style, is the means by which forward-moving action can be controlled. A play is, or should be, a monolithic structure.

This at once presents an absurdity, as the interpretation of a play in performance is carried out by a director, designer and company of actors with individual personalities. The theatre in the last fifty years has become dimly aware of this. It has tried to deal with the problem by group theatres, or ensemble playing. In England nothing much has come of it, except the theory. The team spirit of the playing field has not found its way into the playhouse. This compromise has been arrived at. A central personality is used, that of a leading actor, and about his personality (often there are two, a man and a woman) are grouped the remaining characters of the play. This is inclined to bring about a complete negation of the play as a form, directing attention on the human personality and not on the action. It has also brought about the Actors' Theatre. Which is the theatre in England today.

The actor's art, being interpretative, must be given content. This content is the text of the play. The character within the play, the part, has a defined personality. The actor has his own personality. The fusing of the two personalities results in the performance. This process is complicated and very difficult, so it is not surprising that an actor's initial approach to the text of a play is almost entirely destructive. He tries to destroy the personality of the character in the play and impose his own. This can be a most alarming experience to a writer newly come to the theatre. The play is arbitrarily broken to pieces and not even put at his feet for examination, but more often thrown at his head. Then, in the later rehearsal period, the reconstruction in dramatic terms begins. Good actors, well directed, will reconstruct within the recognised intention of the play. Bad or lazy actors will reconstruct according to a formula which has served in the past. When the first happens any dramatic form, no matter how complex, will work. The personalities and technique of the actors become absorbed in the action. Use the formula, and the actor's personality, not always as interesting as he believes it to be, will predominate.

Preoccupation with this kind of virtuosity has now become an obsession. Shakespeare's plays provide a remarkable opportunity for its practice. Not one person in a hundred, and that person is usually very young, is concerned with what happens in *Hamlet* or *Lear*. They know. Their concern is with what the actor will do. That is putting it at its highest. At its lowest it is a concern with what he has for breakfast or the colour of his bathroom.

A sad parting of the ways has occurred between the playwright and his interpreters. To the writer, drama is a basic form: the theatre is a toy, an ingenious piece of machinery. It exists for the interpretation of plays. To many actors and directors it has become a thing in itself, tiresomely dependent on some form of content. Actors have not yet reached a point in their art where they can merely be. They still have to do something. This is more expertly attended to in the New York theatre. For every play, that is, a work written for the theatre, there are half a dozen fabricated plays. These are adaptations from novels, memoirs, even films, made not with the declared object of being a statement in dramatic terms, but merely as material for performance.

The gravest handicap in playwriting today is the narrow limits within which a play is assessed. The criterion by which a play has come to be judged is its power of conviction as a reality. This was a natural development in a theatre entirely concerned with illusion, and the *trompe l'oeil*. Now it has reached a point where the theatrical is not just mistaken for but accepted as the dramatic. This has led to a cheapening of all dramatic effect.

These limits are often set by criticism. I mean newspaper reviews. That is all I can mean, as modern theatre scholarship of any serious kind does not exist. This criticism only recognises plays in performance. The interpretation of plays is judged usually on complete ignorance of the text. It would be unusual for music criticism to be written without a knowledge of the score. The argument of dramatic critics is that they can only concern themselves with the play in the theatre, as that is the final intention. Yet the intention of music is also public performance.

Let me say that by writing in this way I am laying myself open to the charge, made before, of petulance. The facts are these. Between 1951 and 1954 I had three unsuccessful plays produced in London. Naturally, my sense of failure was acute. I am on the defensive. Very well. If it is a consideration, discount it against what I write here. Now, let's get on.

The development of the theatre must finally rest with the dramatist. Only he can set the course and define the boundaries. An interpretative art, such as acting, can never advance beyond its immediate material; at most, it must content itself with a sharpening of technique. Nobody talks about an *avant-garde* in acting.

A playwright must not think that he will extend his audience beyond that of the novel or poetry. It is a mistake to see the theatre as a popular art. It may have been fifty years ago, but new mediums have changed all that. The play must now be directed towards a specialised audience. That may very well be the theatre's salvation. Physically, it is having to pull in its boundaries. Within a few years it will be in a state of final siege in the West End of London. In all ways it must become smaller, but more concentrated. The question of its constitution at the moment is not important to a playwright. A speculative theatre, such as the English have today, appears at first glance to be a jungle. Yet the German theatre, highly subsidised and organised as it is, produces less native playwrights than we do. Anyway, commercial managements have not been timid in the last ten years. They have done many plays with limited appeal. Most of them, certainly, have been imported from America and France, but that is natural as they have been the best plays. The business of the theatre is a bore.

Perhaps, and this is not a sudden thought, the play is not capable of much development. The ideas, yes: the form, no. And the form, as we see, is all important.

The rise of the curtain. The point of entry into the action. The argument. The development. The conclusion. The whole formal conjuring trick. Everything must be subordinated to the illusion. If it is not, there is a feeling of unease, of embarrassment. And the question becomes, Are we in a theatre? When the answer is definitely, yes, the reaction is immediate flight. A trick has been performed, but it was not the trick that was expected, or, more accurately, the trick that has come to be expected. The audience must be taken out of themselves, their attention must never be turned in upon themselves. Or so it seems. That is what an audience wants. What do the playwrights want? It might be interesting to find out. And then impose it. Henry James began to write for the theatre with an earnest endeavour to appeal to 'the cosy, childlike, naïf, domestic British imagination'. He ended, after five years, with the words: 'It has been a great relief to feel that one of the most detestable incidents of my life has closed.'

For, when all the negative arguments have been put and accepted, when the subject has been discussed and the methods have been agreed upon, after all this there remains a doubt. Isn't it really only a game for the young? To have

STATEMENT FOR A PLAY

(Undated)

I want to achieve something very raw: not coarse in texture, no, raw in the sense of the agony of an exposed nerve. As such it must carry at its beginning the sob of pain, the half-laugh, and then, in progress, rise through the crescendo scream to a finale of realisation and awe.

The whole must have a brevity of expression and a considerable sense of pace. I must remember my newspaper readers. I must hold the man on the bus between his starting point and, yes, beyond his destination. The incidents of the play must flash to his mind as well as to his eye with the urgency and frozen drama of a news picture. Speed, clarity, simplicity of expression and motive – remember this, Never wait for effect – this time, *pace* H. J., throw overboard the cargo to save the ship. Never pause for an audience's realisation: never! But repeat – again and again if necessary – a boxer hitting monotonously in the same vulnerable spot. Find that spot – find the nerve centre of the play and then hit it – hard! and keep on hitting.

The action and motives must be real, very much of today. There must be no element of fantasy in behaviour, place or in names. (Exception: Serafin.) Use real place names, newspapers, radio programmes, political leaders, political situation. I mustn't use the literary reference at *all*. (Start by cutting any thought of epigraphs: or, if I must have one, then take one from the *Daily Express*.)

Build barely from the beginning. Allow the action to provide its own impetus. It will – that is, if it's good enough. Build, moreover, on very general factors of atmosphere. Heat, cold, hunger, repletion, thirst, sweat, violence. Keep it to that.

Keep a line – a steel thread – from beginning to end. *Do not deviate*. No digressions for the building of character, so-called, for the moment of atmosphere or for that moment when you can show what a clever fellow you can be. Work on the principle that the cutting of one word will throw the meaning – the *meaning,* not the rhythm of a sentence. I mustn't build consciously dramatic peaks. Let them come. Don't worry about how someone comes on or goes off – don't worry, that is, as to whether it fits. Let them come in or go off, and if it makes a balls of the surface don't worry – let it tear into the surface – let it stick out like a sore thumb.

Write it fast. I must set a time when I'm ready to begin, and then down it must go on this bloody machine and I mustn't stop until it is down to the last word in some kind of shape – any kind of shape – but let me get it down.

Keep it exciting. Just keep it exciting and I'll be all right. Give the sense not that it might happen, that it could happen, that it's going to happen someday – give the sense that it *is* happening.

Whenever in the writing the thing begins to stick – whenever there's any doubt as to what happens next – get on with the story.

Remember the man in the bus – he hasn't got time to hang around listening to arguments – he hasn't, poor devil, got time to listen to poetry for the sake of poetry – he hasn't many strong allegiances – he's got to get on – where, God knows – but he has a job and he's forgetting every day how to relax and there's a war coming too. So get on and attract his attention.

Remember the man on the bus. Forget theatrical technique. Forget what you've learnt and remember the audience. Think of how to attract an interested if ghoulish crowd in the street.

Forget one thing: J. W.

How to put it down. Words. Ordinary: brief: caustic: (a styptic pencil applied to a pimple): funny if you like but contribute to the story.

Get on the inside. Don't use even the smallest property which you can't now get up and fetch and touch – feel its weight, its warmth, its shape. Try not to use any phrase which you haven't heard – actually heard. (Forget your 'wonderful use of language'. Language is dying – hopelessly perverted – then use that perversion to bring home certain facts.)

Get on the inside. Remember what you have learnt. It doesn't matter what it looks like on the page. It can't be balanced in the writing as you thought. (It can – you will allow no one the experiment.) Balance the dialogue. Look through the conventional plays. Just put it down – that's all.

Just put it down.

FROM A NOTEBOOK (2)

(1960)

There is a lot of talk nowadays about new stages; the things on which plays are performed. And every time, whether the platform concerned is set in an arena, or is a forestage, a space stage (whatever that may be), or a guess at an Elizabethan stage, a word always crops up. The word is 'intimacy'. This, I take it, means a close emotional and intellectual contact between actor and spectator. It is always thought to be a good thing. Is it?

I suppose it is part of the times. We huddle together in life, and seem to think that we shall understand better if we lie in each other's laps. So it is natural to believe that an actor will communicate more if we can stretch out and touch him.

But, my God, there is power in the remote, isolated figure neither giving nor asking for understanding or love. Isn't it, perhaps, the power of the theatre, to which a return must be made sooner or later? I may be wrong. We shall have to wait and see.

❖

The purpose of art is to raise doubt: the purpose of entertainment is to reassure.

❖

I've been looking through photographs of Duse. The actor's face. It must have love and it must have pride, it seems. They are basic qualities which Gielgud can transform to aching loneliness, Olivier to threatening decadence, Evans to tumult and Tutin to comic defiance.

Ah, the tragedy in the theatre of a noble mind behind an insignificant, amiable face. The man can putty it over and paint it up, but we're never taken in. On the other hand, there's the tragedy of the insignificant, amiable mind behind the noble face. They exist. Dear me.

❖

The effect of television plays on plays written for the theatre has become very apparent in the last two years. The philosophy of television, and its criticism, is to treat everything in terms of a newspaper human story. This is a natural development with television dominated by journalists, which is right and proper, for the thing is visual journalism. Television plays occupy that space which newspapers give over to dogs and babies. A glance, a smile, a tear, are all that are required.

It is when this approach is applied to the play in the theatre, with its deeper implications and need for a more formal pattern, that confusion begins.

The theatre is the only art which lacks an articulate form of scholarship. So it is always being mistaken by its audience for something it is not.

❖

A West German audience. A thousand coats left in apparently unlimited cloak-room, to reveal the men's hard double-breasted suits and the women's tea gowns. In the theatre. Heads towards the stage as if in clamps. No talking. Controlled laughter. Deep attention. Never a sign of boredom, as far as I can see. Yet it must be so sometimes. In the interval. A little walk. A soft drink. Back in their places without fuss. Grey faces against the inevitable grey theatre. Three such performances on consecutive nights recently. Then, on the fourth night, to *The Gypsy Baron*. It was like a safety valve.

Paris. Usual seediness of surroundings. Heads turning all about as if they had got in the place by mistake. Everyone knowing everyone else, and showing it. Nobody appearing to have paid. (Has anyone ever met the person who has paid for a theatre seat in Paris?) Usual arbitrary start to the performance, as if someone has suddenly lost his temper and is imposing the play as an act of penance on the audience. Curious impression that the people who get up at the end of the play are not the same as those who sat down at the beginning.

London. A thousand raincoats draped over a thousand knees. Much reading of the *Evening Standard* before the play begins, and as much afterwards as the light allows. All as restless as the sea. The English cough. The American tourist who has lost the thread of the story. The pretty display of cigarette lighters over programmes whenever a new actor enters. And in the bars and corridors, between acts, much loud, articulate and savage criticism. Angry faces, mostly women, who seem to have been insulted. Men bored. But they all sit it out to the end. Dramatic critics sometimes pretend that members of the audience leave during a performance. This is not so. These people are going to the lavatory, attempting to move to more favourable seats, or buying the limited number of things available by law in a theatre. They do not leave the building.

❖

In all great performances in the theatre there is something sacred. Yes, I've been reading Malraux.

❖

I was in a very bad temper this morning: ended by laughing at myself. I'd picked up a newspaper in which a lady said that something I'd written was old-fashioned. How touchy we become, and how prickly at certain words of criticism. I'd never heard of the woman (you see?), but I read her article with an intensity far beyond its value.

Funny. We don't mind being called scoundrels, and we get a warm feeling when we're said to be a menace to society. But suggest that we don't know our job, or that we're out of touch with the great big world and we begin to chatter.

There is Lifesmanship in criticism, as in everything else. I've learnt to evaluate it for what it is. Pity it's a one-sided game, though. I could play it back at some of the boys and girls very well.

❖

A long conversation with an American student on the influence of present-day American playwrights on their English counterparts.

Ended in great doubt. Can anyone trace the sources of influence in playwriting, as is possible in poetry and the novel? Not at the moment, I'd say. And that perhaps explains the weakness of so many plays. They have become inbred.

I was told recently that a group of playwrights meets at the Royal Court Theatre every Wednesday to drink coffee and discuss work in progress. Now this is undoubtedly untrue, and is just another of those filthy things which are said about that place. But the fact that anyone could think up such a lie is indicative of the way playwriting is seen nowadays. For it's true that many plays give the impression that they have come into being by a kind of cannibalism. Each play devouring the one before it. And then presenting itself in innocence.

Ten years ago I deplored the theatre's dependence on literature. Well, that marriage broke up. Since then the theatre's been sleeping around with journalism, reportage, propaganda, autobiography and the movies among other things. And the old whore's produced some very odd offspring. I must leave it to Americans to sort out the genealogical confusion.

❖

Thought of the plays that have made me laugh (intentionally) in the last ten years. Ashamed to put down the list.

❖

Is there a great store of unperformed English dramatic literature? We're often told there is, but nobody is very specific about it. Taking the four hundred years between 1500 and 1900, each decade seems to have produced one play that might be revived. This, as in most other arguments, excepts Shakespeare. The eighteenth century makes up for the dearth in the nineteenth century. Forty plays. A couple of years repertory. It's not much.

All this after finding some Massinger and Tourneur unreadable.

Can the bravest theatregoer among us really stand up and fearlessly say that he looks forward to the National Theatre's productions of Byron's *Manfred,* Tennyson's *The Promise of May,* Lytton's *Money,* Garrick's *Miss in her Teens,* and Cibber's *She Would and She Would Not?*

❖

That terrible moment in the theatre when the first actor steps forward, opens his mouth, and you know it's going to be *all wrong* from beginning to end.

❖

Talked with an actor about 'his career', as he put it. I felt like a very small donkey he was preparing to ride to Parnassus. Actually, he was only going to appear in one of my plays.

❖

About to do a new play in London. Usual hallucinatory state. Wish for instant flight. Nightly dreams about remote places, broken by harsh, unforgiving laughter. I move among friends like a sick man. Frenzy when newspapers get the title wrong, or misspell my name, or confidently say the play is set in some impossible place, or is about what it is not about. Dread of first reading with a row of actors with unforgiving faces, perched, as I always am, on a chair which for two or three hours seems on the point of collapse. During rehearsals a period of terrible bravado, leaving in its wake many unintentionally insulted people. The first night. This time I shall go and kiss the actresses, and then have my dinner, making it last just as long as the play.

There are stories of playwrights who stride into the theatre on the first day and read the play *to* the actors. These men are said to sit in Row G on the first night and laugh at their own jokes. They give interviews to newspapers and when the newspapers get them wrong they write letters of correction. They appear on television and shout down all opposition. They answer their critics. They write furiously.

It is a comfort to know that their plays sometimes fail.

❖

I saw by the young man's face that he was very distressed at my flippancy when I talked about the theatre. I tried to make amends, but it was no good. He walked away.

I suppose I do care very deeply about the theatre as an art. After all, I've spent most of my life in it. Of course, it's surrounded and sometimes dominated by more nonsense than any other art. And the only defence I've found against this nonsense is ridicule. Unlike other people who write plays, especially the young, I have no sense of mission. I state what I believe to be true, but I don't try overmuch to convince. I suppose I'm old-fashioned (see above) in that I'm concerned with form. I've written half a dozen plays now, and the technique no longer concerns me. I leave that to my critics. I'm only interested in taking a subject and extending it to its absolute limit, within my own experience. But that's all any of us are about.

❖

The play can be a remarkably pure form. I find it strange that so many playwrights now introduce song and dance. Or is it the directors? Historical precedence is often invoked. Am I the only person who reaches for his hat when the actors begin to chant and hop?

❖

Fallacy: that any art is infinitely communicable to an unlimited number of people.

❖

There are times when anyone writing for the theatre longs for the control over performance that a score and the presence of a conductor dictates in music.

A line in a play holds just so much sense and no more. Just so much emotion and no more. It's when an actor begins to invest a line with meaning or emotion which it doesn't hold that this control is so necessary. The really great actors exercise their own control. They give a line an essential rightness of sense, which makes it seem impossible to read it any other way. They also make the emotion a kind of atmosphere in which the sense can freely exist.

Lesser talent often tries to over-humanise. This nearly always results in a breakdown of the language, and a reaching out towards a false reality which becomes promiscuous.

AT EASE IN A BRIGHT RED TIE

(1959)

Mr Gaitskell, who wore a bright red tie and a large red
carnation, spoke persuasively and was at his ease throughout.
Report in the *Observer,* July 12, 1959

I am not a Marxist.
Karl Marx, towards the end of his life

The main engagement took place in Sloane Square. There
was a complementary action in the far east, at Stratford. These
separate forces were never co-ordinated. The east relied very
much on mercenaries recruited from another country. The
west, although at one time there was an uneasy and short-
lived alliance with France, employed the natives. The west
once occupied the Palace and the Comedy, but these were
not held. At this moment the east has taken Wyndhams and
the Criterion. The situation is now confused. What exactly is
written on that banner which the winds of expediency will so
irritatingly fold? What are those charming businessmen doing
on *this* side of the barricades? Is it true that some of the
insurgents have been decorated by the enemy? They say the
social-realists and the experimentalists have fallen out. There
are ugly rumours of unholy alliances. Even the citadel itself,
the curiously named Royal Court, is threatened.

Come home, Ken Tynan!

It is permissible, I think, to write in these terms, for we
have been told so often that what has happened in the theatre
is a revolution. The theatre is a small world, the revolutionary
theatre in particular, existing as it does in two centres and
between the covers of this magazine.* The failure of such a
movement need not cause great concern, but for one thing: it
reflects the failure of a whole way of thought among young
English men and women today.

A revolutionary movement should have some reasonably
defined principles, but it was never easy to understand the
common cause which bound the Royal Court Theatre

* *Encore.*

playwrights. They undoubtedly understood each other, but their dissension often seemed frivolous to an observer. Of course, the Left has always believed that public argument within its ranks is a sign of virility. There is the famous story of Lenin and the man of the centre, and there are the recent Labour Party statements to prove this. Such behaviour has considerable entertainment value, but it is doubtful if it has ever produced a sound political idea. It has certainly failed so far to produce an influential theatrical movement.

One thing was clear, however, and the playwrights engaged in the Royal Court group were definite about it. Their political philosophy was socialism. This usually had to be gathered from personal statements, as the political ideas in the plays have rarely strayed beyond the parish pump. All these writers, with the possible exception of Mr John Osborne, who has the universal appeal of misanthropy, were firmly committed to parochialism. This, of course, was not admitted.

The danger in revolution is not losing, but winning. By a successful revolt the movement puts itself in power and so relinquishes the possibility of further revolt. Revolutions can only evolve beneath power, never downward. It is this simple fact which more than once has embarrassed the Labour Party. Are the fruits of revolution always conservative?

Something of the kind seems to have happened in the recent theatrical revolt. There is a sudden awareness that the natural evolution of man, even revolutionary man, may be from radical to conservative. The idea, which is by no means new, has caused great despondency. Again, I must assume this from conversations, and more especially from a curious little article by Mr Arnold Wesker in a recent issue of *Encore*. In this article Mr Wesker poses a problem in semantics on the comparative meaning of the words reaction and response which is quite beyond my understanding. But Mr Wesker also writes this sentence: 'Free Cinema has come and is going, the attendances at the Universities and Left Review Club are dropping, the faith people have had in a theatre like the Royal

Court is gradually being lost, and the men and women who spoke to us two years ago with such concern and intelligence are now bored with our company and our groups.' This is certainly the voice of disillusion.

Mr Wesker's absentees can be divided into two groups. The first is made up of people who will hang around when any fight is going on in the hope of seeing someone get hurt. They sometimes believe that by cheering and booing they are engaging in dispute. They are not, but it is a fair enough game. The second group is composed of people who were genuinely sympathetic to the ideas and progress of such things as the Royal Court, Free Cinema and the ULR*. The absence of this group is the real concern.

The defection has occurred in the last two years, Mr Wesker suggests. In that time we have seen the decline of socialism as a political ideal in Western Europe, and a contempt for all that it stands for. Two men, de Gaulle and Adenauer, have made a mockery of the whole structure of republicanism. The French Socialist Party has demonstrated once again the danger of riding the tiger. Weak, good-hearted and foolish, it has been eaten up. The German Socialist Party has been revealed as a cipher, an invention, a sop to liberals. There has been the failure of both black and white democratic forms of government in Africa. Internationalism, outside the expediency of a military alliance, has died on its feet. Here in England we have the less violent but no less frightening possibility of trade union delegates being recalled after a conference resolution to vote and vote again until the answer comes out right.

Everywhere, faced with the conflict between principle and policy, socialism is backing policy, and losing.

It is against this background that we are asked to accept and approve the plays which are put before us by young socialist writers.

The dictum, 'It is not enough to be simple. It is not even enough to be what simple people call good. The simplicity

---

* Universities and Left Review.

of a darkened mind is no better than the simplicity of a beast,'
applies perfectly well to politics. I am not suggesting that the
writers under discussion are ignorant, but I do suggest that
their minds are darkened in the theological sense.

Their concern with humanist values is admirable, but it
is so often expressed merely by a sort of kindness,
Saroyanism, as it used to be called, which is not enough.
Their criticism of class distinction is more applicable to
feudalism, and not the highly complex society in which we
live today. And their sympathy for minorities and the
under-privileged is apt to become sentimental, and end up
with no more than the handing round of tea and buns in
St Pancras Town Hall.

The supreme problem of socialism has always been that
it is essentially a militant philosophy which is largely
committed to pacifism. This apparent contradiction has
sometimes made it appear foolish, and sometimes simply
inert. It is not a new problem. It has exercised individuals
and split parties for a long time now. I can find no mention
of it in any play written in the last four or five years.

It may be said that the theatre is compelled to present its
conclusions more in terms of feeling than of reason. But if
this is so it must not assume a didacticism beyond its powers.
Large claims have been made for the Royal Court movement
by critics such as Mr Tynan, not merely for artistic
achievement but for such matters as social reform and change.
The movement must expect to be judged on those claims.

I do not underestimate the difficulties facing these writers.
They are working at a time when the influence of the art of
fiction in both the novel and the play has declined.
They may have the zeal and social passion of Zola and
Dickens, but their instrument has far less effect. A live two-
minute television interview is often more revealing than the
most exhaustive reconstruction in fictional terms. All the
same, it remains factual and inconclusive. The power to
reach and present conclusions is the writer's sole prerogative

over mere reporting. The Left Wing writers completely fail to understand this.

In the matter of style the movement is largely committed to realism. Reality, I suppose, may be defined as applying to any one person all that comes within that person's experience. For example, the spiritual experiences of a saint seem to many a form of fantasy, but to the saint they are reality. The substitution in literature of the bed-sitting room for the drawing room, and the dustman for the duke, is not an achievement for realism. And an insistence on the universal realities, such as eating, drinking and making love, is only tolerable if such things go on, as they do in most people's lives, in a wider context.

So, with their failure to come to grips with the political philosophy they profess, and working in a style which is deteriorating into the most trivial reporting of fact, these writers can hardly expect the revolution to continue. Set against a play such as Mr Robert Ardrey's *Shadow of Heroes,* their work seems tame, but at the same time shrill. It is interesting to note that Mr Ardrey's play caused little stir in Sloane Square circles. Yet this play, attempting a documentary style far removed from realism, with its dialectic, its passionately cold concern with the problem of allegiance to an idea, was perhaps the only truly political play we have seen in this country for years. Why was it ignored? It would be unkind to suggest that it was too explosive to be touched by our home-made revolutionaries. Equally unkind to suggest that their liberalism made it impossible to recognise the play because it was produced in the West End by a commercial management.

The struggle at the Royal Court and elsewhere, it would seem, was for the theatre to take on a greater social and political responsibility. Crying Forward, it is dwindling from our sight. Plays are being produced which rely for their effect on a false naivety. The problems they present are being simplified to a point of non-existence. We face the prospect of having nothing in this kind of theatre but plays for peasants. Mr Osborne uses his considerable power of invective to wither things that are unimportant. Socially, the whole way of thinking is out of date. And, I say this without malice, out of touch.

From the political point of view the movement means nothing at all. Like the leader of the party, it seems content to wear the proper symbols, so that it has always looked right. (I mean, of course, that its appearance was correct.) And the movement was a heart. No doubt about that. All the throbbing emotionalism proves it. We are asked to admire its virility. I am pleased to do so. It is that little tiny head which worries me.

CRITICISM

GEORGE BERNARD SHAW

(1956)

I cannot write about Shaw from personal knowledge. I met him once, when I was a schoolboy, and I was quite overlooked. I last saw him in the early days of the war. I was on leave, and window-shopping in the sun along Piccadilly. I became aware that the reflection in the glass was not a small white cloud, but a long white beard. He was standing beside me looking with approval at some thick woollen garments. Then, as if remembering that he had little time left to loiter, if he ever had, he was gone.

He was, of course, most fortunate in his choice of appearance. I can never remember what people look like. But from these two brief glimpses of Shaw the whole man comes to the mind's eye. It must always have been so. From the early days, with the clothes of a revolutionary and the devilish red beard and moustaches, to the later days when the beard became patriarchal and the flat caps gave way to curious pot-shaped hats.

Well, he is dead now, and what has he left to a generation which is apt to think of him as a funny old man?

This is an age of timidity, when an act of generosity can seem like bravado, when we are afraid to say or touch anything for fear it goes off. Shaw had a habit of hitting things with a hammer to see what happened, and, using the written word, he trampled down with the greatest kindness.

The criticism which has been directed against him since his death is tiresome, if for no other reason than that he said such things about himself, always more accurately, and with a great deal more humour. He was probably the first example of the now common muddle about the artist as entertainer, reformer or general meddler in others' affairs.

He saw himself as reformer, pamphleteer, and as a permanently angry man. The plays were the means to this end. In spite of his attitude, the plays are the work of a great artist. We are made aware of an argument, but it is the argument of a man, not of a sect; of a single human voice, not the crowd. He was a virtuoso, with Picasso and Yeats, the great example in his time of the supremely unselfconscious artist.

The man in the plays seems curiously vulnerable. The failure of the early years, and terrible it must have been to him, was treated by him as a farcical incident to the end of his life. That was his own particular dishonesty: it can be forgiven. As a man he had much in common with Byron. The love of friends, the lack of cant, the self-mockery, the pain which set off laughter. Both were men one would like to have known well. Men who can catch reality, like a bullet on a plate, and show us its harmlessness. Both are best known for their follies, and both are most suspected by the English for their brilliant sincerity. To be accepted, sincerity must be monastic, mute and dull. Byron died too young. The other dirty trick was played on Shaw. He lived too long.

For the time being the plays seem unreadable. Shaw knew this must happen. In 1903, he wrote: 'To younger men they are already outmoded; for though they have no more lost their logic than an eighteenth-century pastel has lost its drawing or its colour, yet, like the pastel, they grow indefinably shabby, and will grow shabbier until they cease to count at all, when my books will either perish, or, if the world is still poor enough to want them, will have to stand, with Bunyan's, by quite amorphous qualities of temper and energy.' Even the single masterpiece, *Heartbreak House,* with its extraordinary overtones of the present time, its uneasiness and chill, does not quite convince. Yet it is the play which will carry the rest through. It poses the questions, but does not answer them. The earlier plays answer all the questions, asked or not, and it is our misfortune, not Shaw's lack of art, that the answers have now become the questions.

The qualities of temper and energy, which he dismissed as amorphous, will preserve the plays, for they are the qualities of good poetry and prose. Probably the last thing he would have wanted, with his contempt for the belletrist, was to be known as a fine writer, but that is how he will stand, for the artist always eats up the man.

Like Shakespeare, his plays will return to us, glittering. We shall wonder, be delighted, and try to remember the circumstances that brought about such gaiety and triumph. Only the very solemn and the very scholarly will worry about that. The rest will accept, as they now accept in Shakespeare, the clear voice of an amazing human being. A most dear man.

HALF TIME AT THE ROYAL COURT

(1957)

When the English Stage Company began its activities at the Royal Court Theatre, everyone was happy. It was, after all, very brave to start a theatre. It is always very brave to start a theatre. The manifesto and press announcements perhaps gave the impression that it was a good cause and not a theatrical venture which was about to be launched, but the wording of such things is notoriously difficult. Some of the associated names may have seemed a little strange, but they were distinguished, even if in other branches of life than the theatre. And, as is known, it takes all sorts to make a management. Mr George Devine was to direct matters. There were unknown names, such as Osborne. Everything seemed for the best.

Well, we have had this new English theatre with us now for over eighteen months. During that time everybody has quite rightly been very nice about it. Even dramatic critics have bounced the baby gently. It has been treated with a seriousness very unusual in this country.

So let us see what we have.

The place seems to identify itself with some not quite identifiable movement. The word most commonly used is 'contemporary'. As this word is used nowadays to cover anything from an art to those funny little objects you are supposed to hang your hat on, it is not helpful as a definition. I take it to mean that the thing has been created recently.

Now certainly the Royal Court has set an astonishing precedent by producing entirely literate plays, and most of them by living authors. This, I suppose, must support its claim to be a modern theatre. But it is useless to look for a unity of style either in acting or production, the factors which surely make a theatre of this kind.

Indeed, the poorness of performance, or to be quite blunt about it, the downright bad acting, is probably the most distressing feature of the Royal Court. There have been some most excellent individual performances given, especially by women, but small parts and ensemble playing sometimes utterly defy criticism. An example was a production this year of Giraudoux's *L'Apollon de Bellac*. This was wiggery-pokery at its most outrageous. Not only was false hair stuck on every exposed piece of actor, but there were also humps, limps, stutters, false noses, false teeth, a whole museum of theatrical absurdity. Beneath this a not insignificant play suffocated.

It had happened before in Nigel Dennis's *Cards of Identity*: it has happened since in Sartre's *Nekrassov*. If someone is under the impression that this infantile kind of ornamentation is a theatrical style, the sooner they are disillusioned the better. The danger is that the thing seems to be contagious. Olivier's performance in *The Entertainer* bore traces of it. Now this mighty actor could probably play with a house on his head, and his virtuosity is so great that it sweeps away such trivial irritations. But an actor who has only a little workaday personality must act and not just disguise himself.

All this gives the ordinary member of the audience, and I am one, the uneasy feeling that the performance is in some ways a private joke. Are they not enjoying themselves just a little too much up there on the stage, and are we not just a little left out of it down here in the audience? God knows, we don't want to be loved, and the English theatrical tradition of sucking up, 'your humble servant', is a dismal thing. The fluency of any great performer rests on his arrogance, his absolute autocracy, and very exciting this can be. But the performances at the Royal Court are not of this order. Too often it is just a chap in a funny hat getting a laugh from his friends.

The greatest achievement of this theatre so far is that it exists. A point of much interest is its future development. It has begun to expand. Productions now appear in Shaftesbury Avenue, Moscow and New York. Sometimes simultaneously. Therefore it is impossible to speak of an English Stage Company in the singular. This policy, I take it, is very necessary from a financial point of view, but surely it has dangers. One is that the Royal Court Theatre, the place itself, may lose its identity. It may become nothing more than the centre of an organisation. Certainly, in the past, classical theatres have made world tours, but they have not in the process thrown up subsidiary companies.

From this arises one main question. What exactly is the English Stage Company?

Is it an organisation for production which happens to have its offices in Sloane Square? In short, has it abandoned its original intention and now gone into straightforward competition with commercial West End managements? And is the English Stage Company nothing more than an out of the way theatre with a label?

Well, many ventures have started with less, so may we please go on from there? And it will not do just to revive *Look Back in Anger*. This is becoming a joke, a sort of intellectuals' *Charley's Aunt* which doesn't just turn up at Christmas.

I know that by writing in this way I may sound like a dramatic critic puffing at a theatrical policy without regard for the practical difficulties. But I am not a critic. I am one of the audience. An audience, moreover, whose disinterest in the theatre has often been deplored by theatre people. They call it an intellectual audience. Let it stand at that. Anyway, to people like myself the reopening of the Royal Court was an event of some importance. Our interest in a theatre of this kind is such that we do not need to be shunted into it by good reviews. We are enthusiastic in our rather strange way, and are prepared to accept a talent such as John Osborne's, an extraordinary talent for the observation and recording of human behaviour, even if we hohum over his political and social views. And we are tolerant. To a point. That point being when showmanship tries masquerading as something more serious, or when windbag controversy starts banging about in an attempt to catch votes or sell seats. Then we get very, very bored.

I may be making a grave mistake. Perhaps the Royal Court is not intended for such people. I have an idea that it was in the first place, but if it is no longer so I shall be sad and I would also like to be told.

'I suppose he means that the only good theatre is the commercially unsuccessful one.'

And the answer to that is yes, in many cases, yes. Reproductions of paintings hanging in the National Gallery are sold by hawkers in Oxford Street for a couple of shillings. They are in nice plastic frames. And I suppose some people buy them, but I doubt if we can congratulate ourselves on the cultural state of the country because of that.

A NEW ENGLISH THEATRE

Roots by Arnold Wesker (Penguin Plays)
Serjeant Musgrave's Dance by John Arden (Methuen)
The Complaisant Lover by Graham Greene (Heinemann)
Raisin in the Sun by Lorraine Hansberry (Methuen)

(1960)

Do you think when the really talented people in the country get to work they get to work for us? Hell if they do! Do you think they don't know we won't make the effort? The writers don't write thinkin' we can understand, nor the painters don't paint expecting us to be interested – that they don't, nor don't the composers give out music thinking we can appreciate it. 'Blust,' they say, 'the masses is too stupid for us to come down to them. Blust,' they say, 'if they don't make no effort why should we bother?'

This is Beatie Bryant speaking up good and clear against the working class (well, what the devil does one call them now?) at the end of Mr Wesker's play, *Roots*. It may be interesting to examine the four plays under review in the light of this outburst. They have some things in common. All adopt the highest moral tone. None of them is purely didactic, and none of them is purely entertaining. All of them seem a little out of date in technique.

Mr Wesker's play, *Roots,* is the second play of a trilogy which is unified by theme, but not by plot. The play is about ignorance. It takes place among farmworkers in Norfolk. The story is very simple. A young girl arrives home to prepare her family to meet her boyfriend with whom she has been living in London. The boy never appears in the play, but his character is described with loving care, and a more nauseating prig it would be hard to imagine. He takes the opportunity of the girl's absence to break with her, and she is left under his moral influence at the end of the play with a mass of misconceptions, half-truths and a general confusion of mind which she expresses very forcibly to an understandably uninterested family.

I am not sure whether Mr Wesker intends the girl, Beatie, to be the most devastating example of a young person seduced by popular culture. I think not, for his sympathies seem to lie in her direction. The last line of the play, for example, is: The curtain falls as Beatie stands alone – articulate at last. Articulate, yes, but expressing as many common fallacies as can be got on to a couple of pages. The girl seems to see art as an educative influence, something which uplifts, does you good. Nonsense! Some of the best art teaches nothing and can do irreparable harm, if not actually deprave.

Mr Wesker identifies himself closely with his characters in that he is a muddled man. He seems to believe that knowledge is revelation, and that art can be a substitute for faith. This is an error which must inevitably develop when man's social state is elevated to a spiritual experience. Mr Wesker has also been made very angry by the discovery that ignorant people cherish their ignorance, will defend it, and even fight for it. And this anger is, in its own way, a kind of ignorance.

Mr Arden writes an introduction to his play, *Serjeant Musgrave's Dance,* in which he carefully tells us all the things the play is not. It is not nihilistic, symbolic or pacifist, he says. I don't know about that, but I do know that the play is a magnificent piece of work.

Mr Arden is unlike Mr Wesker in that he is concerned not with how people live, but with what they are. It would seem to be a much sounder basis for a work of literature.

A winter landscape. A northern town in England, eighty years ago. Four soldiers are apparently on a recruiting campaign. Actually they are deserters bringing home the body of one of their comrades killed in a colonial war. From this simple material comes the most amazing play. Musgrave himself, the divine anarchist, is a frightening creation. Austere, brutal and compassionate, at once recognisable, he dominates the action. Through him Mr Arden achieves that most elusive emotion in the theatre, genuine rage.

If Mr Arden can write like this for the theatre he really must stop worrying, like one of Mr Wesker's characters or a dramatic critic, whether the play is *about* or *for* anything. So there is no need for him to introduce his next play with such humility. If the theatre is for anything, then it is for plays of this kind.

Is the theatre for Mr Graham Greene's plays? Yes, if they are as sadly funny as *The Complaisant Lover*. This play holds a personal vision just as intense and vivid as Mr Wesker's or Mr Arden's. But it deals with a subject they have yet to tackle. They write about love. Mr Greene writes about sex.

It is the story of Clive Root, an antiquarian bookseller, and his love affair with Mary, a dentist's wife, and the amiable, if forlorn, arrangement reached by the three of them.

The play does not miss a thing. It is as sour as the taste of a not very well-known mouth in the dawn hours, as dry as dust under an hotel bed, as formal as the first position, and as inconclusive as any furtive encounter.

If you want joy you must turn to Miss Lorraine Hansberry's *A Raisin in the Sun*. It is full of it. Sickeningly so. Actually this play is Victorian melodrama which has somehow got put down in Chicago, and all the characters have turned into Negroes. Thirty years ago they would all have been Jews. What they will be thirty years from now is anybody's guess. But one thing is certain. The play will be written again round about that time. It has been appearing regularly for the last hundred years. There seems to be no reason why it should not go on giving good service.

Hard-working wife, small child, no-good husband. Pretty sister. Mama (to whom the play is dedicated) is a monument of selflessness, wisdom and work. Large sums of money are gained and lost – but need I go on? Cheer up. All ends well in poverty but pride.

Here, then, are four plays produced in the English theatre in the last year. And in the light of Beatie Bryant's remarks quoted above how does the scene look?

First of all, it seems that the theatre must, in spite of Mr Wesker, give up trying to be a popular art. Mr Arden also suffers from a delusion in this respect. He seems to be under the impression that by including ballads in his plays he is working in a form immediately comprehensible to the dimmest intelligence. *Serjeant Musgrave's Dance,* however, turns out to be one of the most sophisticated plays written in the last ten years. But, of course, it is not important what means a writer like Mr Arden uses, if the result is as fine as this play.

Another lesson to be learnt from these four plays is that it is very unwise to be fooled into thinking that the technical skill of Mr Greene, or for that matter, Mr Rattigan, is an empty thing. Of the four playwrights above it is Mr Greene who has chosen the most universal theme. This is probably why the play had the longest run. It also demonstrates the fallacy that a work of art appeals on the level of class, education or upbringing. It does not. It always has and always will appeal on the level of experience. For example, *The Complaisant Lover* would probably seem to be not only a horrid, but an untrue piece, to a young man or woman. But to someone in middle age it has more than veracity, it has its own kind of poetry.

It would be a pity if the theatre, which is an enchanting thing, were to fall entirely into the hands of the zealous social reformer. There is a danger that this may happen because since the war, England seems to have bred a generation of morbidly serious young people. Their spokesmen, and Mr Wesker is one, seem to believe that plays, and indeed any art, are a means to an end. This is not so. They should exist in their own right. The question, What is it for? is always an enquiry made by an illiterate. The Beatie Bryants of this world should go to teachers, text-books or, probably most effective, church. It is a serious matter to lead them to believe that they can short-cut things by playing Bizet on a gramophone record, hanging prints of Van Gogh on the wall or by going to the theatre, as Mr Wesker seems to believe. There is a way out of the desert of provincial English life, but this is not it.

I happen to be writing this in Vienna. The theatres and the churches are full. The sun is shining, and there is not a work of social significance within striking distance. Has this prejudiced me? Probably. I will read Mr Wesker's next play sitting under the trees in Sloane Square. In the rain.

Meanwhile, let me make a suggestion. All English playwrights under thirty should slowly and carefully write out the following words by Thomas Mann before they begin work each day: 'A work of art is something which is worth doing for its own sake.'

INSIDE THE ASYLUM

Stop It Whoever You Are by Henry Livings
(1961)

It is always interesting to come back to England and find out what is making the people laugh and how they are trying to frighten themselves to death. For the English have always needed a circus and a bogeyman to keep them happy.

For the past few years the theatre in this country has provided them with both. It has now reached a state where it is so remote from life that it is like a modern Bedlam. Within its enclosure, strictly defined by its conceit, pomposity and self-importance, tumble the playwrights, the actors and the critics. At its boundaries, occasionally, stand the English people. They hear cries of argument which they do not understand, a lunatic goes fooling past pretending to be one of them, another is making a long speech. All is confusion and very very private. I am reminded of this by one or two things.

First by Mr Henry Livings's play, *Stop It Whoever You Are*, recently at the Arts Theatre. After the first performance of this play there was a comic shiver of horror. The play form had sunk from that sensible object, the kitchen sink, to that useful, if dull place, the public lavatory. Now Mr Livings's play is truly funny, if a bit untidy and thoughtless. But it is not enough that it should be funny, it must be shocking and degrading too. So the puzzled audience and newspaper readers, on hearing and reading that a lavatory is such a dreadful place, shrug, turn away, and conclude that the lunatics must have very odd ideas. They have. And very innocent ones, too. So that as well as being absurd they are rather touching. Touching in the way that an angry baby sits in a corner and mutters the word 'bottom' to itself, and believes it is putting its immortal soul in peril.

The other day I was stuck in the traffic in Piccadilly Circus. In the distance banners were bobbing above the heads of an orderly crowd. The Nuclear Disarmers were being safely shepherded into the Haymarket so that they could sit on the pavement somewhere. Now I am sure that within that tight group, so neatly contained by policemen, there was passion, faith and hope. But none of these things was communicated to the people around me. It was a private war. And, most tragic of all, the demonstrators seemed happy. It is this happiness, this smiling idiot face, smug in isolation, which makes the theatre so negative a thing in modern life.

Government by power, especially in Western Europe, has always been aware that literature is a weapon. Forced by circumstances to practise a mock liberalism towards such things, it no longer insists upon suppression. It is content with a policy of containment. The artists have made this possible. Drunk with the thought of freedom they are content to demonstrate within the cordon.

Authority smiles on the arts. It does not subscribe anything, but it smiles. A new Sunday newspaper of uncompromisingly right-wing views employs a dramatic critic who in another place has expressed a political philosophy of a very different kind. Why shouldn't they employ such a man? He can't do much harm outside the asylum writing about the theatre. Trapped in his column, his sad face peering out at us through a little window, he is that all too common sight nowadays. The liberal man in search of a political leading article. What has he got? That joke, the theatre.

The *Lady Chatterley's Lover* case* took place inside the asylum. Liberal opinion tore itself to pieces in the Old Bailey. I was outside the asylum at the time. One morning during the last days of the case I went into a pub. It was a fine day. The place was quiet. One man stood at the bar. The barman was reading a paper. He asked: 'What's the dirty four-letter word in this book?' The man thought. 'Beer?' he hazarded. A joke, which would have been quite beyond the comprehension of the defence witnesses, had passed without laughter between two men outside the madhouse.

---

*DH Lawrence's novel had been banned for thirty years. Penguin published it illegally in 1960.

Such tiny bones of contention, such as the printing of Lawrence's novel, are often thrown our way. Not to keep us quiet, for the noise is tremendous. Marching and countermarching in the name of freedom we achieve massive victories for minute trivialities. Lawrence's novel can now be sold in sweet shops. All the same, it effectively distracts us from using our time for more dangerous matters.

Alienists say that the mad have no sense of the past, and the future is nothing but a vague foreboding to them. This seems to apply, frighteningly, to many young dramatists. Contemptuous of history, terrified of the future, trapped within the limitations of birth and death dictated by humanism, they are transfixed in the time they like to call the present. And on this fine edge, which does not exist, they attempt to create works of art.

These men are even shy of using normal terms concerning their job. If, when they come before the public, which is often, such a phrase as 'a work of art' should slip out, it has to be apologised for, laughed away. The desire for the commonplace has become so great an obsession that it is now an affectation in its own right.

So we have this curious situation. Dramatists writing plays, actors performing them, and critics reviewing them; all being done in a private world. The mania reveals itself when you examine statements which are always being made on the subject. These people believe themselves to be stridently engaged in life. Reality – these words! – is the new mythmaking substance. Fix it with absolute accuracy and it will transcend itself to the point of revelation. That is what many people in the theatre believe. So do madmen.

It seems impossible for this silly state of affairs to go on much longer. So there is hope.

One day, and surely it must be soon, everyone in the theatre will be forced into their proper senses. They will come to understand that their job is not concerned with scoring points off each other, it is not internecine war. God knows, nobody asks that an art should be polite or concerned with

ONE AND ONE MAKE ONE

Loser Wins by Jean-Paul Sartre,
translated by Sylvia and George Leeson
(Hamish Hamilton)

Lieber Gott, mach' mich fromm, dass ich nicht
Dachau komm! *German children's song, circa* 1933

It was necessary to invent a hell so that prayers could be said
asking salvation from our own creation. The need still exists.

M. Sartre's most recent play, *Les Séquestrés d'Altona,* of which
Loser Wins is the English version, takes place near Hamburg
in the present day. Old von Gerlach, head of a huge and
prosperous shipbuilding firm, has six months to live. He is
dying of cancer of the throat. There is the question of succession.
Werner, von Gerlach's younger son, evades the acceptance of
responsibility, as his wife, Johanna, evaded it in her earlier
career as a successful film actress.

The existence of hell is revealed. It is an upper room of
the house. Franz, von Gerlach's elder son, has shut himself
away for fifteen years. As an officer in the German army he
committed an act of atrocity against partisans on the Eastern
front. Still wearing his uniform, sitting with a tape recorder
beneath a portrait of Hitler, he addresses and questions his
judges and court of appeal. The court is composed of
imaginary crabs. Oyster shells litter the floor. Primitive and
predatory life fills the room like a stench. Franz is dedicated
to the perpetuation of a fallacy: that the Allies have imposed
on Germany economic and social conditions of such
harshness as to reduce her to absolute and permanent ruin.
Franz's belief is encouraged and his ideas confirmed by his
sister, Leni, who serves and looks after him, and with whom
he has an incestuous relationship.

The resolution of the play is brought about by the invasion
of Franz's solitude by his brother's wife, Johanna. This foolish,
incompetent and ordinary woman, in a struggle for power
with the sister, is the means by which Franz comes to accept

the truth: Germany's present authority and prosperity. The exquisite vision of ruin, 1945, fades. Franz comes down into the house for the first time since the war, and confronts his father. In a brilliant concluding scene the two men meet. Guilty, accepting, arrogant and utterly impotent, they are incapable of judging each other. They grope for some authority to condemn them. There is none. They leave the house together to kill themselves. Franz's voice, from the tape recorder, makes the last statement. Werner, the younger brother, and his wife, both vacant with irresponsibility, wander away. Leni, the sister, goes to the upper room to take Franz's place. Someone must occupy that room, she says. The need for punishment, for hell on earth, is perpetuated.

Germany, between 1934 and 1945, has become a romantic image for Western Europe, more especially for the sophisticated societies of England and France. Newsreels of the period, shots of the leaders, the rallies, and especially the brutalities such as the concentration camps, take on an almost poetic quality. France, as open as a wound since 1945, has been most infected. *Les Séquestrés d'Altona* is saturated with this new romanticism. Scene after scene pays homage to it, and the attitude of the characters is dominated by it. Even in incidents, as when father and son commit suicide at 112 miles an hour over the Teufelsbrücke in a Porsche, it almost absurdly conforms.

Von Gerlach, Franz and Leni are all conceived in this romantic tradition. The two characters who are not, Werner and his wife, are treated with something near contempt. This is all as it should be, for today the criminal is the heroic figure, the man who has acted to an extreme is the concern. The personal gesture is everything, the comprehensive and humane gesture is nothing.

The play is very frightening in its statement of despair.

We act, and by acting we commit the crime. We are aware of our monstrous indiscretion. We long for judgement and punishment. We face our judges and at once the position is absurd, for they are as guilty as we are. We implore their condemnation, but they will not speak. They are aware of the counter-charge. So accused and accuser stand face to face in impotent silence, both asking for conviction from an authority which does not exist.

The judgement is absent. Can the crime be made so awful as to bring the longed for retribution? We have tried very hard in the last thirty years. We vie. Hitler filmed the conspirators of July 20 strangling to death on meat hooks, and ran the movie for his friends' pleasure. Not long after, the newspapers printed photographs of those friends hanged at Nuremberg. The number of dead in the extermination camps was being drawn up at the time of the decision to drop atom bombs on Hiroshima and Nagasaki.

The ordinary man examines the monsters, a Hans Frank or a Heydrich, and cries in wonder, But he's a man, like me. There is comfort in the understanding that we are all capable of great crimes. For if it is not so, then we are innocent, and so lost. We elevate the mass executioner, and then search history for circumstances which created these gross and cynical men, believe we find the cause, and affirm: We are guilty. The judges laugh. So are we, they say.

This ridiculous dilemma is exquisitely laid out by M. Sartre in his play.

Franz's voice from the tape recorder speaks these words in the last minutes of the play: 'The century might have been a good one had not man been watched from time immemorial by the cruel enemy who had sworn to destroy him, that hairless, evil, flesh-eating beast – man himself. One and one make one, there's our mystery. The beast was hiding, and suddenly we surprised his look deep in the eyes of our neighbours. So we struck. Legitimate self-defence. I surprised the beast. I struck.

A man fell, and in his dying eyes I saw the beast still living – myself. One and one make one – what a misunderstanding.'

The play has unfortunately received a most misguided production at the Royal Court Theatre, in a translation by

Mr Justin O'Brien. It is produced under the title *Altona*. This is rather like writing a play about Jews and calling it *Hampstead*.

There are many difficulties facing the director of this play. Mr John Berry, who is responsible in this case, has managed to solve none of them. The play is of great length for one thing, but the cuts which have been made seem arbitrary and rather hysterical, and make complete nonsense of some of the continuity.

The play is done in a setting by Mr Sean Kenny. It is theatrically effective (although it would be nice if someone put the swastikas the right way round), but manages to make the von Gerlach family look poor. The set has none of the hilarious ponderousness of the Krupp house, which it is surely supposed to resemble.

The actors, with one exception, seem at sea. Miss Diane Cilento elects to play Leni, the sister, with the enunciation of a musical comedy tenor. She manages to insinuate herself round, over and under Mr Kenny's set in an extraordinary way. The small, neat figure, a model of German thoroughness and fanatical purpose, which is delineated by M. Sartre, quite escapes Miss Cilento. This is all very strange, remembering some of Miss Cilento's performances in the theatre. Striking in appearance, and with a distinctive personality, she rarely subordinates the part to these qualities, but she has done so in this case. She suffers a great disadvantage, however, by being referred to by everyone in the play as Lenny.

Miss Claire Bloom, as Johanna, seemed decided to take no part in the proceedings, as she obviously considered them insane. She treated every other person in the play with the tenderness due to the sick. She brought a solid air of common sense into the place. The last thing that was wanted.

Early in the play, von Gerlach is referred to by his children as old Hindenburg, and it is said that Bismarck was still alive when von Gerlach acquired his habits. This is a traditional figure, surely easy to recognise. The Prussian philosophy froze such men into tragic and pathetic postures. The meeting in the 1920s of these men and the new German produced some fine examples of high farce. Examine photographs of Hitler and Ludendorff together in Munich. The younger man is trying to ape the older in fixity, while Ludendorff is making democratic efforts to loosen his neck. And both are filled with self-contempt for their play-acting.

Mr Basil Sydney, who plays von Gerlach, does not attempt the colossus. He is not, as he should be, a nineteenth-century monument unaccountably stricken with a mortal human disease. He is a member of the present-day managerial class all too understandably irritated by an ulcer. There is a point late in the play when his son Franz asks: 'There isn't a God, is there?' And von Gerlach answers: 'I'm afraid there isn't. It's rather a nuisance at times.' This beautiful, calm and ironic line is said by Mr Sydney turned away, as a muttered apology. The actor at this point becomes the English puritan on the run, not the German Protestant he should be.

The exception to a basic misunderstanding of the people in the play is Mr Kenneth Haigh as Franz von Gerlach. The part is one for a virtuoso, and Mr Haigh takes it as such. It is very exciting to see an actor in the English theatre who is possessed of real passion and, what is more important, can use that passion to illuminate sense and meaning.

There is an idea in England that any prolonged self-examination, especially in so public a thing as a play, is an indulgence. It is called self-pity. Mr Haigh has fortunately never subscribed to this view. He sets out on the vast uncharted areas of self, disappears, emerges again in laughter, worries at details, turns about, advances, retreats, comments, and is both bored and fascinated by this creature he is portraying. He does all this with great effect in M. Sartre's play. He conducts before our eyes a relentless investigation of the character, and when, at the end, he finds it worthless and throws it away, he is most moving.

The hopeful will look in vain for any confirmation of their ideas in this play. M. Sartre speaks from the continent of Europe, and with a voice which has no equivalent in England.

Therefore it must fall a little strangely on our ears. The pulse-rate of this country has always been low in such matters as are dealt with in this play. We have always been a little incredulous of a man who *acts* in political faith. Some of us believed that the Englishman's attitude to European politics could never be the same after 1938. We were mistaken.

However, this play may be of more than academic interest to this country in the near future because one of the things it deals with is the ruthless methods needed in this century for the survival of the individual.

A GOOD LAUGH

Beyond the Fringe

Alan Bennett, Peter Cook, Jonathan Miller
and Dudley Moore

I suppose every good comic must be an affront to us. He must offend our modesty and self-respect. I don't mean that the insult must be to what we believe, to our faith or morality, but he must try to capsize our sense of rightness. Then we shall laugh.

The open insult can be small in itself. There was Groucho Marx's cynical greasepaint moustache, and Harpo's preposterous wig, both making an open declaration of falseness. These were effects. There was W C Fields's contemptuous and casual juggling. This was an attitude. And there is the circus clown's disregard for material; working within narrow limits he charms by his degree of perfection.

Comedy is anarchic. Once it saddles itself with the order which is inherent in belief it fails, or at least becomes something else. Chaplin has shown us this over the last twenty years. Being anarchic, comedy must be dangerous. When it plays safe, you get the recent decline in the theatre and literature.

All comedy is amoral. It is a process of destruction. It is something we have to protect ourselves against, or we shall die laughing. We live from day to day with a growing belief that all institutions are absurd, but we try to keep straight faces. We must, or we shall end the world. We are thus compelled to define our objects of ridicule with care. Invariably they are objects of power, things that we fear. War, military matters generally, death, government, all these are fair game. But turn the ridicule towards the abject, the poor or the persecuted and the open laughing mouth becomes an abyss.

There is every reason why life should be taken seriously, yet life persistently refuses us the means. Actions of the gravest consequence, such as war, revolution and famine, are invested with an element of farce by the men who precipitate them. Bertrand Russell appears on television. He is asked if he thinks many people will join him in sitting on a pavement. Yes, he says. He thinks there are at least five thousand people in this country who don't want to be blown up by a hydrogen bomb. Joke, we scream, it must be a joke. A new movement is formed. It is called the Anti-Violence League, and is for the reintroduction of flogging. Joke, surely a joke. Dr Verwoerd* speaks of good neighbourliness, President Kennedy of being threatened by Cuba, Eichmann of how his auntie came of really quite nice people. We believe our ears. We fall about.

It is no longer possible to equate laughter with happiness. A definition of the word *amuse* is: to divert from serious business. But laughter is now a serious business, concerning itself with serious things. We cannot now even equate laughter with amusement.

The conscious practice of this art, the power to cause laughter, has become very precise. Like other weapons it is now refined to a point of delicacy where we fear an accidental explosion. We have been able to protect ourselves in the past. Time has transformed *Gulliver's Travels* into a children's book, and the same process is now at work on *Animal Farm*. We are lucky that the effect of humour, although instantaneous, is of short duration. Also, its impact is local. God help us all the day when a man turns up who makes the whole world laugh.

The little Fortune Theatre, which nestles in the armpit of the big Drury Lane Theatre like a bomb, went off the other week. Four brilliant men, Alan Bennett, Peter Cook, Jonathan Miller and Dudley Moore, were the cause. The explosive charge was their material, devised by themselves. The revue is called *Beyond the Fringe*.

It is an extraordinary experience. It would be unwise to call it an entertainment. Arrogant, impertinent and arbitrary, it is devastatingly funny. Like Groucho's moustache, no attention is paid to conviction on the lower levels. All impersonations by these four men are done without physical

* Prime Minister of Apartheid South Africa 1958-66.

aids, mainly in flannel trousers and schoolboys' blue jerseys, or at most pressing into service a filthy raincoat or a clerical collar. Properties for one scene are left lying on the stage for the next. No scene ends, it merges imperceptibly with the next, and for no other reason, it seems, than that someone has been left on the stage. This gives a joyous continuity which is very rare in this kind of production.

There is no dancing, unless Mr Miller's convulsive movement can be seen as a kind of dance. Everybody is trying to describe Mr Miller at the moment, so let me try. I think he was drawn by Mr James Thurber some years ago. Striding forward, hand outstretched, he tries to stem the bursting dam. At rest, he sits huddled, no, bunched up, as if high on some small piece of furniture. But this man, like all great comics, is elusive.

There is no singing, except for some savage masculine bursts of sound in chorus, and Mr Dudley Moore accompanying himself on the piano. He gives us a fragment of lieder, and a setting of *Little Miss Britten.* They come to us with the fading charm of the Third Programme picked up by the car radio late at night on country roads.

No singing and no dancing. This will come as a nasty shock to people who have been going to revues in London during the last twenty years. Indeed, there are none of those deliberately produced *longueurs* in *Beyond the Fringe,* such as the sentimental song, the period *pastiche,* or those antics called dancing.

There are some twenty-four sketches in the revue. One of them, called 'Bollard', fails, not because of its execution, but because you can see the pay-off from the start. All the rest, not having pay-offs anyway, succeed splendidly. Very wisely, nobody has seen fit to comfort us anywhere during the evening. Neither the eye nor the ear is allowed to rest. On the contrary, there are two moments of variation, and these are not achieved by softening up the proceedings, but by an excursion into extreme violence. The first begins with a casual conversation on the mutual tolerance between grammar school and public school. The words peter out into uneasy silence. This silence is broken by a quiet voice, saying 'Of course, you know Jonathan Miller is a Jew.' Miller squirms on the hook. The others walk away. Moment of total irreconciliation. The other scene is set in a death cell. It has a violence to the sensibility which proves that what theatrical managers call bad taste can, if taken to such a limit, become the purest form of social comment. This sketch is the revue's 'Modest Proposal'.

These two diversions seem perfectly successful to me. During the whole evening we are never treated to the theatrical equivalent of those political cartoonists who make us laugh week after week, and then, letting their feelings get the better of them, suddenly turn out one of those embarrassing drawings of starving Negro children, or an emaciated refugee. The cast of *Beyond the Fringe* knows exactly where its talents lie, and what its job is. It is done to perfection.

There is one doubt. Is a theatre, as we know it, the right place for this kind of thing? The same difficulty came up recently in the London production of *The Connection*. This play was nearly destroyed by the bad acting, but much of the failure was due to the fact that it was done in the *wrong place*. *Beyond the Fringe* does not suffer from being in a theatre, but it is diminished. Many people are concerned with round, square and oblong theatres. It would be nice if they would put a little time aside for designing a building suitable for this kind of revue. And when the cast of *Beyond the Fringe* has done with it, let it be handed over to that other comic genius, Mr Spike Milligan.

There is an advertisement in the programme of *Beyond the Fringe*. Now you must see *One Over the Eight,* the hit revue, it says. Duke of York's Theatre. 'Scandalously funny' – *Evening News.* 'Snappy and gay' – *Evening Standard.*

As I am devoted to anything which is scandalously funny, and in constant search of the snappy and gay, I went along.

Beyond the Fringe opens in studied silence. Mr Moore comes on. He plays 'God Save the Queen'. We rise. So do the cast. Mr Moore goes. We sit. Mr Miller asks: 'Who is that man who keeps on coming on and playing "God Save the Queen"?' And we are away.

One Over the Eight opens with nine people, the company as they are properly called, coming on and singing words which are inaudible and playing on musical instruments made of wicker. And we are nowhere. In spite of the fact that the ninth person is Mr Kenneth Williams.

This is revue as we have long known it. The steely, fixed smiles. The clothes which haven't been worn since 1923. All performed by real gals and fellas. The programme has a drawing of a chap drinking bubbly.

There is lots and lots and lots of dancing, *and* singing. The dancing is of the meaningful kind. The singing is the loud kind.

That desperate man, Mr Kenneth Williams, is almost submerged in the goings-on. The drunken oboe player which he keeps inside him and uses for a voice sometimes interrupts the proceedings. There is a moment when the dancers desert the stage – one can only suppose they are lying exhausted in their dressing rooms – and Mr Williams creeps on alone. He instructs us in bird-watching. Passionately crouched in his rotting tree stump, glaring around, he becomes that eternal object of fascination, the obsessed man. But it is only a moment. The dancers have recovered and returned. Mr Williams is lost in the company, the finale, and the wicker instruments.

Hope springs early in the evening when Mr Williams interrupts the prancing, grinning figures. Still as death, bitterly aggrieved, he asks what is going on. For a moment I thought all this mediocrity had been assembled only for Mr Williams to be able to dismiss it, and that the horrible settings had only been put up so that he could pull them down. This done, I believed he would consider us contemptuously, capitulate, and, sitting in his rotting tree stump, talk to us for a couple of hours about this and that. But it was not to be. Mr Williams capitulated to the company.

Now I must reveal what I can only suppose to be a sinister joke. The sketches in *One Over the Eight* are credited to a Mr Peter Cook. We must suppose, for sanity's sake, that the Mr Peter Cook who has written much of *Beyond the Fringe,* and so brilliantly performs in it, is a different man. If he believes himself to be the same then he must be disillusioned at once.

THE KITCHEN

(1962)

The Kitchen, recently produced at the Royal Court Theatre, is
Mr Wesker's first play. It is a fine piece of work, brief and
vivid, with an energy which some of us found lacking in his
recent plays. There is nothing more wearisome than assessing
one play against another, and so I resist the temptation to
call this Mr Wesker's best play. All the same, it should be
said that *The Kitchen* is startlingly different from *Chicken Soup
with Barley, Roots* and *I'm Talking about Jerusalem* (the Wesker
Trilogy, as it has come to be known, which inclines us to
approach it on the same emotional level as The Gospels.
Or the Forsyte Saga).

The action of this play takes place in the kitchen of the
Tivoli Restaurant within one day. With great subtlety Mr
Wesker has allowed the formal activities of such a place to
dictate the dramatic shape of the play. It is morning, and a
single figure enters to light the huge ovens. As they roar into
life, the other workers, chefs, cooks, kitchen-maids and boys,
butchers and waitresses, arrive. The climax of the first act –
the play is in two parts – comes with the hectic rush which
occurs with the serving of lunch. The second act begins and
proceeds in its early part with the afternoon lull, which one
supposes must happen, below and out of sight, in large
restaurants. These scenes of the play have a lyricism which
I have never before found in a play by Mr Wesker. The over-
hot kitchen, the undressed cooks, the fragmentary and
revealing conversations, all, place, people and method, are
used with great yet economical effect. Mr Wesker has also
understood the element of fantasy, which in moments of
relaxation seems to be invested in places which are devoted
to prosaic activity: a factory at night, an army at rest or, as in
this case, a restaurant kitchen in the afternoon. He allows
this fantasy to possess his characters, so that the men and
women we have seen in the early part of the play preparing
and serving food with a maniacal concentration relax into

private worlds, which shift and interpose to form a quite extraordinary dramatic effect. The play ends with a scene of violence precipitated by an emotional crisis of one of the characters. At first sight this seems arbitrary. It is only in retrospect that the ingenious *form* of the play becomes apparent, and that the form is poetic in nature.

Mr Wesker has rejected any idea of conventional structure. He has dismissed the dramatic notion that a play rests on a firm central theme or situation played out by a few main characters and supported, often as an expedient, by a number of less important people, such as maids, neighbours or first and second lords. It is true that *The Kitchen* has a dominant story. This is the demented love of a German cook for a young, married waitress. And it is this situation which brings about the tragic end of the play and reveals Mr Wesker's cunning. For let there be no doubt about it; he knows what he is doing when he lets the whole social organization, the skill, labour and blind activity to feed us, be brought to a complete standstill by the misery of one man. In the last moments of the play, the workers in the kitchen stand silent and shocked as the bloody figure of the German cook is taken away. Social man, and the servers of social man, are at a standstill both in awe of, and homage to, the agony of an individual. At this point Mr Wesker very rightly ends the play.

The Kitchen has a rare quality in that it is about people doing a job. And what is more, they do it in front of our eyes with complete conviction. Their work becomes part of the drama. A conversation, an argument, or a declaration of love has to be broken off because somebody wants something to eat. This has an immediate truth: it must occur to many people, say in the middle of making love, that they ought to be doing some work. It rarely seems to occur to characters in plays. Here it does, with both comic and tragic effect.

There are thirty characters in the play and every one, however small, is made real and compelling. The wary, and I am one of them, are inclined to mistake Mr Wesker's lack of cynicism for sentimentality. It is a mistake the most well-meaning person might make in this day and age. But in *The Kitchen* there is a tartness of observation concerning human behaviour which makes such an error of judgement impossible in the future. Let me give an example. At one point in the play the German cook embraces his waitress. Mad with love, he raves on about immediate elopement, escape to romantic places, the sea, the sun and the ski slopes. The girl leans back in his arms and says, 'Well, 'smatter of fact, I can't. I'm having my hair done tomorrow.' This is so chilling a comment on the bitches of this bitch of an earth that one can at last forget Mr Wesker's eternal question, Why can't we love each other? For he has answered it himself in this anecdote.

It may be that Mr Wesker intends us to see *The Kitchen* in a wider context, that is, as a kind of allegory. The characters are of many nationalities, and the conflict between them is often racial and ideological as well as personal. They become united only in the moment of common labour, which in this case is getting my dinner. So, if it is intended, the allegory fails because I am sitting upstairs waiting to be fed, and the play does not take me into account. But the play would fail on such a level for a less trivial reason. And this is because the people in the play are so interesting in their attitude towards work, so very often moving in their acceptance of life that any more formal or philosophical reason they may have for behaving as they do is lost in their fascination as *people*.

Mr John Dexter's direction of the play cannot be too highly praised. From the moment the ovens purr into life at the opening of the play to the moment of stark madness at its end, all is under the most unobtrusive control. There is no falsity, no straining for effect. Both play and actors have been treated with love and care. Mr Robert Stephens, as the possessed German cook, and Miss Mary Peach as his woman, give performances of wit and precision. As does Mr Harry Landis. The others, and there are too many to mention, give uniformly excellent performances.

In a conversation after the play, it was pointed out to me that this production was a first-class example of *ensemble,* or company, performance. We have heard a lot in the last few years about the need for this approach to production which is basically a uniformity of style of acting within any particular performance.

A common error is to suppose that this style can be imposed from without the play, say by the director. This is not true. The play itself will dictate the style of performance. So the following dilemma arises. A permanent company dedicated to a style of acting might well play *The Kitchen* and yet be hopelessly at sea in *Camino Real.* This can be overcome by the degree of virtuosity of the actors forming the company. But the greater the virtuosity of the individual players, the less likelihood of an *ensemble* performance. Unlike *The Kitchen,* most plays are, and have been for thousands of years, written with the central and exceptional characters dominant (what actors call bloody good parts) and the lesser characters subservient. (Actors' reference to these parts is usually unmentionable.) The truth is that the play is a hopelessly undemocratic form. It exists on an outdated social philosophy which says that every man (or actor) should know his place and stick to it. As I think I have demonstrated above, *The Kitchen* is an exception. But the excitement generated by Mr Dexter's production should not lead to any false hopes for the future.

To get back to the play. Or rather to Mr Wesker.

He is reported in an interview earlier this year to have made the following statements: 'One of the reasons why *The Kitchen* was so successful, in its own way, was that it was written at a period when my experience of the theatre was very limited, and I did not have anybody at my elbow saying "You can't have a play with thirty-two characters... you can't do without an interval... you can't have ovens on a stage", and so on,' and 'Now, let me tell you something very distressing. I am finding that art is beginning to have no meaning for me – it is not enough. To have to sit down and be cold and calculating about a piece of music, then organise a dramatic work to *say* something, is like organising a murder. This is obviously a bad state of affairs.'

It is, indeed.

First of all, *The Kitchen* as a work of art makes complete nonsense of these damned silly statements. Mr Wesker seems convinced that because he asked for thirty-two actors and some ovens on the stage in this play, he was breaking some kind of convention. Like all socialists, he is obsessed by material things. But as the very considerable artist he is, he should have learnt that very small people – and he is not one of them – will always be at his elbow warning him what *not* to do. He should ignore them.

As for the second statement, Mr Wesker is conducting in public that private struggle which has occupied us all at one time or another, the conflict between the moralist and the artist. Most of us, if history has left us any fragment of humanity, feel that we would be better occupied in the refugee camp, the hospital, or (Mr Wesker's favourite activity) sitting on the pavement outside the Ministry of Defence than putting words on paper, or paint on canvas. But in Mr Wesker's case it is a temptation which should be resisted. He should put aside his scruples, take his courage in both hands, be cold and calculating, and commit for our benefit another crime like *The Kitchen*. And while he is engaged on it, let him remember that it is as difficult for a writer to be a *reasonable* human being, as it is for him to be a gentleman. The thought may cheer him up.

But I am pontificating. And Mr Wesker will be laughing at me. So I'll shut up.

LUTHER

(1961)

Little Monk, you have chosen a difficult path.

There is a new puritanism about. The idea is heavily over-subscribed in the theatre.

The way of thinking seems to go something like this. Plain speaking must be the order of the day. The equivocal is suspect. Wit causes distraction: cleverness is a blind for some sort of corruption. Colour and glory dazzle, or worse, confuse. The virtues of courage and humour are more than absurd, they are useless. There must not be two sides to a question. Basic needs must not be elevated; food is matter for evacuation, not energy, and sex must stay rooted between the legs. How long will it be before we hear again the ridiculous term 'natural man'? Not long, if things go on at this rate in this direction.

The younger and more intelligent dramatic critics deplore the corrupt ceremonies of the theatre at the moment. Many of them have reacted strongly against the genius of M. Anouilh. His artifice is thought to be shiftiness, his negligent wit unhuman. He is not down to earth.

The perfect exemplar of that deplorable position is Martin Luther, about whom there is a new play.

This disgusting peasant, filthy in word, mind and body, a kind of human sewer, did more harm to Western Europe than any other man. Graceless and repulsive, he blundered into history on his knees, brought there by a clap of thunder, his bestial superstition, and fear for his safety, both spiritual and physical. Elevated far above his capabilities by ignorant and commercial interests, he was given to making pig noises against authority. But when authority moved against him, he became as servile as a sponge. Gifted with the sense of timing which is possessed by second-rate actors, he stood his ground only at expedient moments. His power of language, often spoken of when nothing else of any good can be said of him, is overestimated. A rabid anti-Semite, he laid ground for the persecution of that race. He is credited with statements so vile, so inhuman, of such excess, that it is hard to believe he was sane.

Luther is a perfect example of the kind of man society vomits up at moments of crisis. Placed in a position where his words are widely heard, such a man begins to believe that he is more than he is. Pressed to acts and decisions which frighten him, he is driven to fear that the social forces which created him will at last destroy him. So he betrays them, as Luther did the peasants, or vilifies them, as Hitler did the German people in his last days. Death for such a man is a mercy. Luther continued to live: the greatest sell-out of all time.

Mr John Osborne has taken Luther as the central figure in his new play.

This is as good an occasion as any to see how Mr Osborne is getting on, so let us take a little look back.

It is only five years, although it seems a lifetime, since we first heard of Mr Osborne. He was borne into sight on the wave of optimism which broke in Sloane Square with the opening of the Royal Court Theatre. The wave receded, as waves do, and Mr Osborne could be seen, floundering a little, as was to be expected, with his play, *Look Back in Anger*.

The play was very coolly received on the first night. It lurched to the end of the first week, seats to be had for the asking. There is a legend in the theatre that it was Mr Kenneth Tynan's review on the following Sunday which made the play into a success. I have recently looked at this article. I am astonished to find it full of qualifications. The play is a *minor* miracle, it needs changes. Mr Tynan gives ten plays a year better notices than this, and patronises every one of them a great deal less.

No, it was not a critic that made *Look Back in Anger* a worldwide success. It was Mr Osborne's talent. And there's no doubt about that.

But although Jimmy Porter's voice continued for many months to speak from the Royal Court stage, Mr Osborne remained a playwright, and had not yet become a 'movement'.

This translation took place the next year with the production of *The Entertainer*. This piece, mercilessly derivative in style, contained symbolism. It was at once apparent that Mr Osborne was not concerned with you and me and Jimmy Porter. He was concerned with England, the Crown, the Church, Democracy, and Socialism. In short, the front page of the *New Statesman*.

The voice of Jimmy Porter was lost. Another took its place. The voice of Mr Osborne himself. He spoke to us by various mediums. He chastised us. We liked that, although we didn't quite understand what we'd done. Snarling (as he would put it) with the anger he had made so famous, he signed petitions for tolerance. Racial segregation, capital punishment and nuclear disarmament were all taken under his wing. We applauded. It's not true, you see, we said, that the working classes don't care.

About this time a small domestic comedy called *Epitaph for George Dillon* drifted across the scene. It was reported to be an early play by Mr Osborne, written in collaboration. It was a delicate piece, concerning itself with the dilemmas of a group of human beings. It soon went from sight. More important things were in hand.

One of these was *The World of Paul Slickey*. This musical play must rank as one of the monuments of ineptitude in the English theatre. Produced by Mr Osborne himself in the style of a 1923 production of *No, No, Nanette,* it rambled on for hours, although not, understandably, for many weeks. It employed actors and singers of a desperate archness. What it was all about we shall probably never know, for the printed version is more incomprehensible than the stage performance.

The most exciting aspect of the whole thing was the out of town opening. Those diligent men, the theatrical columnists, sent daily, almost hourly, reports. They spoke of frantic cutting of a five-hour performance on the one hand,

and manly efforts to shore up the financial arrangements on the other. Strange American ladies, undoubtedly an invention of Mr Osborne, made statements. We began to wonder if Mr Osborne's real talent didn't lie outside the theatre. In the circus, for example.

By now we have become used to a management presenting not a play by Mr Osborne, but Mr Osborne.

The play which recently opened in London is called *Luther*. Mr Osborne's name outside the theatre is in letters of the same size. A quick glance: John Osborne by Luther? Surely not.

All the same, whatever the play is called, and whoever it is by, it has been widely praised. Although I've yet to meet anybody who likes it. And let me say at once that this is not Mr Osborne's fault. He has laid out a method of production in the text of the play which is concise and clear. But the play has been *produced*. For example, in the printed version Mr Osborne starts the play with one man simply and straightforwardly speaking to another. In the stage performance the play begins with a lengthy celebration of mass, or some such nonsense. Again and again, the text of the play demonstrates what is wanted, and always the production ignores the instruction or deliberately clouds it.

When you are up against it with a playwright, you can always admire his use of language. Let us do so in this case, but with a reservation. German is a fine language for scatological reference. English is apt to squeak under the pressure, as it does in this play. Mr Osborne's transcription of Luther's diatribes more often than not produces a long whistle, when it should bring forth a German fart.

But it is very difficult to judge a play when it has been so criminally mishandled as in this production. We shall have to wait until Mr Osborne's sense of loyalty deserts him, and he moves house.

Beyond criticism, in the right way, is the magnificent Albert Finney as Luther. Here is a man who breaks the conventions of his art with an easy assurance and complete confidence. I remember I first saw Mr Finney as a student some years ago in a play by Schnitzler. He came on stage dressed in evening clothes. He proceeded to blow the play to pieces, and in doing so literally burst out of his costume before our eyes. At the end, white waistcoat and boiled shirt hung about him. It was an involuntary symbolic act which caused great satisfaction. It is to Mr Osborne's credit that Luther's gown manages to contain Mr Finney.

Well, that brings us up to date with Mr Osborne. I was hoping this would be merely an interim report, but news received from the south of France seems to indicate otherwise.

It is sad that we shall have no more plays from him. If he could learn to whistle in the dark like the rest of us, it might be possible. Still, let him be content. *Look Back in Anger* was a masterly expression of an age and generation: *Epitaph for George Dillon* was underestimated (that other hand always worries me); *The Entertainer* gave a fine part to our best actor; *Paul Slickey* was a disaster; and *Luther* remains unproduced.

Yes, let him be content. It's not bad going for any playwright over five long long years.

SOME NOTES ON ACTING

It is strange that with the extension of the art of acting in the last fifty years by film, radio and television no real attempt has been made to define the different approach needed for each of these mediums.

The general attitude of the profession seems to be that acting is acting, whether it is by stage, screen or microphone. This is true, I suppose, inasmuch as it is all the interpretation of dramatic material. Actors are aware that technical differences exist and that material dictates a method of interpretation. But I have yet to meet one who *thinks* differently on the stage, the film and television. He may exist in numbers. Difficult to find out. Very good actors never seem to talk about their art. Very bad ones never stop.

❖

The influence of the shape and size of an actor on the reality of the part. The very pretty girl. She is clear and concise, obviously knows her job, and all should be well. And yet – the performance does not quite ring true. We search for means to explain this, but often overlook the purely physical aspect. Is it not sometimes that she is just too pretty, or not quite pretty enough?

Hofmannsthal writing to Strauss about the casting of *Der Rosenkavalier:* 'Oh well, if all basso buffos are long and lean and only the Quinquins thick and fat I may as well close down.'

Why do all the young actresses have flat a's nowadays? It's very fashionable. They turn them out of dramatic school like that.

❖

The matter of training actors. This is something which is going to concern not only the theatre but the whole acting profession in the next few years. The dramatic schools do their job, and by and large do it well. It is the next stage in the proceedings which causes concern – the period between being an adolescent student and a mature actor. This time used to be filled in by provincial repertory, but with these theatres in such decline where does the actor go? What usually happens is this. The young actor leaves the drama school and, if he has any discernible talent at all, is at once offered work on television. From then on he must complete his learning as best he can. And it is not easy for him. Professional producers for the stage and television are not teachers. The actor is forced to learn by trial and error.

It would be a good idea if commercial television were to establish a kind of postgraduate school where young actors and actresses could continue their studies while earning their living professionally.

Am I being naive? Not really. Television eats up, digests and evacuates actors, as it does material, at an alarming rate. Many of the well-known faces that we see, so beloved at the moment, will soon pass on to become publicans, grocers, salesmen or mothers-of-four. Television should think more seriously about replacements.

The problem for the theatre is more complex. An O'Toole or a Finney is rare: these men who seem to leap from the cradle fully equipped in technique, intellect and imagination. The theatre continues to rely on the 'good' actor. And it is his talent which must be brought to maturity.

How? Schools attached to theatres?

These have been tried in the past and failed. As places they seem to breed dissension. They should be tried again: at the Royal Court, Stratford-on-Avon and the Old Vic. The money and the staff must be found. The situation is absurd.

❖

'Les actrices tendent à ajouter au début de vos phrases des "Ah!", des "Oh!", voire des "Mais" et des "Eh bien". La netteté leur fait peur. Elles tendent à envelopper votre texte de ce même flou dont "la femme" aime à envelopper sa personnalité, par répugnance pour l'objet vrai. A se chercher des points d'appui, hors de votre texte, sinon en lui, comme "la femme" cherche des points d'appui à sa vie, et, si la réalité ne les fournit pas, se les fabrique de toutes pièces dans l'irréalité.' – *Montherlant*

❖

I've been reading Charles Marowitz's book.* I thought The Method was dead, or at least discredited, but here it is again in no less than 168 pages. And every word of it will make sense to the converted, even if to nobody else.

Staggering assertions: 'Gielgud is a talented actor who constantly inverts his talent because of a basic misconception of what the theatre is all about.'

Juvenile arrogance: 'I do not subscribe to the opinion that Gielgud is simply "a voice". He is much more than that.' (What, one asks, is Mr Marowitz? Or rather, who is he?)

Superb mumbo-jumbo: 'Here, however, the opprobrium of Indication is lessened because in bolstering the genuine moments in an actor's performance, it serves as more than a mere expedient. Here it becomes a useful auxiliary. Utterly functional, operating on a level which is clearly beneath that of the best work, it remains *organically* second-rate; which is to say, capable of instantaneous graduation.'

There is, of course, a chapter entitled, 'Enter Mr Brecht'. But, when all's said and done, these Method people have at least *attempted* to define the apparently indefinable technique of acting. Not very successfully, but the struggle is there. Brecht spent years explaining *Verfremdung,* and his disciples are now explaining his explanations. All remains as dark as night.

I'm not quite sure who Mr Marowitz's book is for. On the cover there is a list of other books under the general title 'Practical Stage Handbooks'. These include works on Play Production, Stagecraft (whatever that may be), Costume, Lighting, Make-up, and Noises and Effects. (Mr Marowitz's book, I take it, comes under the last heading.) All this seems to point to the fact that the book is intended for the amateur movement. This makes for hilarious possibilities in the old church hall on a Saturday night.

The Method as Means by Charles Marowitz. (Herbert Jenkins)

Vicar: Emotionalism is never analagous to the degree that one feeling can serve another.

Bank Clerk: The death of a puppy does not stir the same sense of loss as that evoked by the death of a mother...

Lady Mayoress: The sense of disgust prompted by an open lavatory is not really akin to the revulsion produced by an unfaithful lover.

Bank Clerk: *The Mousetrap.*

There is a delightful section in the chapter 'The Character of Characters' in which the work of a Method director (American) and a British producer are contrasted. The Method director, a beautiful, sensitive figure, works with a kind of sentimental delicacy which might produce *Kings of Kings*. The British producer on the other hand, is a brutal fool, obviously wearing a hat and with dirty fingernails, and not understanding at all the finer feelings of his players, as he shouts, 'Move down left, dear. No, down *left*!'

Is Mr Marowitz a director? He's American, it seems.

❖

An actor's way of study is as private as his sexual habits. Usually more so. I can find no published account by an actor of his method. And yet it is probably true to say that in this initial approach, at home, alone with the text of the play, lies the actor's genius, and the moment of true creation.

There is a general belief nowadays that a play is created, rather as a social act, at rehearsal. This is not true. The play is formed as a whole at rehearsal, put together by direction from the parts created by the actors from their dramatic material.

I'm sometimes taken aback to find the very limited means an actor uses in study. Too many of them today, especially young men, find their raw material at the bus stop. The observation of behaviour is a very small part of the business. Actors seem to be the only people who refuse to draw on other arts. They insist on relating the part only to their own experience. The reading for the playing of a part is as necessary as for the writing of it.

❖

The extension of the art of acting appears to be unlimited. But it must extend by its own vitality, and not be forced into grotesque shapes by fashion.

❖

Is it wrong to believe that Shakespeare cannot be played with a 'common' accent? This has nothing to do with snob ideas. There is a school of thought which seems to believe that by coarsening the very formal language a humanising effect is reached. All is brought closer to the people. But although the people of Birmingham speak as they do in Birmingham, they become uneasy and aware of a sense of wrongness when they hear this going on. There is a formal speech which has nothing to do with class. God, how the theatre is beset by these absurd and shifting values.

Experiments in other countries? I don't know. Racine played with the accent of Provence?

THE POPULAR THEATRE

There is a sense of innocence in those theatres where coach-loads of people roll up, pour in, roar, and pour out again. Mr Brian Rix's* mug under a flat cap at the Whitehall Theatre; the nice, sexless voices of *Salad Days;* the automatic *Mousetrap* at the Ambassadors; *My Fair Lady;* all these things have a quality very hard to define, but which is at once apparent, even if you arrive on foot and not on a bus. Yes, thinking about it, I'd say the nearest you can get is a sense of innocence.

It is a direct, if debased line, from operetta. This can still be found in glory in Germany and Austria, very rightly so, and the buses roll up there, too. The curtain rises, and Putzi once more meets Mutzi, or Edwin, who is of course the son of a Prince, has once again fallen in love with Sylva, who is a noted nightclub singer. The plot is kept on the boil by Boni and Stasi, and we are away. The clear bright voices ring out, and we are put back into a youth which never was.

It was in Munich, I think, some time ago that I came across a production of a Johann Strauss operetta which some idiot had tried to stage in a modern style. The result was disaster. Fortunately, neither singers nor orchestra seemed much affected by the ridiculous costumes and settings. The music blazed through, and all was well.

Conservatism is the life-blood of the popular theatre: radicalism its death. Clever young men must not be let into it. It carries too high a purpose for mere experiment. It has a curious faith all its own which must not be tampered with. Fine examples, the art at its best, can still be found. At the Teatro Sistina in Rome is a piece called *Rinaldo in campo*. It is splendid. I staggered into the street well after midnight having seen only the first act which went on for over two hours. This act alone contained a fine belting tenor, comics, revolutionary songs, animals, mountain scenery, knockabout, love, patriotism, and culminated in a puppet show and chorus. There was also an actress in the lead who made our young

* See page 155.

ladies of the English theatre look very pale indeed. Starting in crinoline and pigtails the complex plot carried her to tight black trousers, shirt and cropped hair. She sang like a bird, acted like an angel, danced, both formally and acrobatically, was rolled about in a basket, had her bottom smacked, fell in love with us, the audience, as all good actresses should, and we fell in love with her. She also took the first act curtain call with great composure. I shall never know the extent of her repertoire because I crept away. Ah, we Englishmen, with our small meals and short plays! What we miss. As I left the Romans were refreshing themselves with mountains of ice cream and going back for the rest of the play.

Of course, far from the glitter of the Teatro Sistina, the solid gaiety of the Volksoper and the tea and buns of the Whitehall, there are other, more remote and infinitely sad places where the popular theatre is found.

It is amazing how many English provincial towns still house desperate little nomadic shows, here today, gone tomorrow. Nobody seems to know where they come from, or where they go. Yet it is a world which will not die. John Osborne recorded it well, with love and hate, in *The Entertainer*.

Strange performances can be found on Sunday nights in French provincial theatre. In these great, echoing, bitterly cold buildings, with stages the size of football fields, tall thin ladies with despairing voices represent La Chaste Suzanne, or something of the sort, and play out hideous comedies of misunderstanding with small, fat, trembling men.

Then again, further afield, there is the very fag-end of show business. One evening last summer in the Camargue, a small boy arrived at the café and stuck up a poster. It bore the face of a tiger, and the words 'Terrible Ménagerie'. This could hardly be called advance publicity, for already the harsh voice of the promoter could be heard on the tannoy speakers through the village. I walked towards it. As I approached, I passed a chimpanzee relieving himself against a bicycle. The white horses were starting, and looking apprehensively at a thunderstorm coming in from the sea. Brilliant lights, hung from the trees, beat down on a little open circus ring which had been set up in the square by the garage. Three handsome, filthy boys were erecting tight wires and assembling a trampoline. A dark, angry woman was shaking a money-box in the faces of the audience, which was very small. The animals were packed in a compartmented truck, set to one side. It is true, there was a tiger. I waited. It was obvious the numbers did not make up a quorum. Nothing could happen with these returns. No nonsense here about the show having to go on. It began to rain. The chimpanzee wiped the drops from his forehead, nodded at me, shrugged. I saluted this Archie Rice of Provence, and walked away.

The business of entertaining the public. What does the public want? Not always to laugh, it seems. An old woman coming out of a cinema, her face blotched with tears, and a ball of a handkerchief still squashed against her nose. She speaks to a friend: 'I thought that was a really terrible film, really terrible. Not a thing to be said for it. Waste of time and money...' Her voice and snivelling go into the crowd. This is true.

Is it to do with our being touched by something we know to be demonstrably true, a fiction, a confidence trick upon our deepest emotions? I don't know.

When I was a small boy I lived in a part remote from theatres. One day a friend, about the same age, that is eight years old or so, came to me and said he had been to a London theatre and seen Lord Nelson on the stage. Weary sophisticate that I was, I patiently explained to him that what he had seen was an actor *representing* Nelson. The boy would have none of this. He had seen Nelson in person. But Nelson was dead, I said. This made no difference. A form of reincarnation had taken place: Nelson was there on the stage. I persisted. I began an explanation of illusion and reality, fact and fiction. This so maddened the child that he picked up a piece of lead piping which was lying by, and struck me on the head so that I fell senseless to the ground. It is a lesson I have never forgotten. And it is a lesson which might well be remembered by those who write for the popular theatre. Fact, reality if you like, has nothing to do with it.

From Lehar, Kalman, Abraham and Leo Fall we have come to the theatre of Bernstein, Loewe and others. There is an increasing tendency to treat subjects which present problems. This may arise from American puritanism. It will not do. We must resolutely refuse to be impressed by the announcement that someone is making a musical from *The Uses of Literacy* or *The Seven Pillars of Wisdom*. We must yawn when we are told that the sexual problems of the young are going to be sung and danced out before us. We must turn away when a *significant* figure appears on the popular stage. If we don't make a stand about this, life is going to become like one of the serious Sunday newspapers. Intolerable. A place where food and sex are classified, where you are told where to go for your holiday, and men bully you into reading this and seeing that. We have, thank God, the silly theatre. Let us cherish it. Some years ago a clamour of voices rose from a certain place against the middle-class dramatists' treatment of the working class. These writers, these indolent fools, it was said, never looked at life. Why did they always make working people comic? How insulting it was to represent the honest artisan as a gormless idiot. With social love working away, these dissenters set about putting people on the stage as they really are. And what happened? The working people represented stayed away from such plays in their thousands. And where do they go? They go to Mr Brian Rix's theatre, the Whitehall.

And what does Mr Rix present? He puts on with loving care a series of farces with such titles as *One for the Pot, Dry Rot* and *Simple Spymen*. Generally playing a leading part himself, he ranges from a North Country simpleton to a young man in direct descent from the Aldwych farces of the 1920s. This may not be a wide range, but it is enough for his audience, which loves him. He has a semi-permanent company (I feel sure that Mr Rix has referred to it on more than one occasion as just one happy family) which has become adept at farce technique. Masters of the double-take, the tea-cup business, the going through the door business, virtuoso on and under a sofa, and of the funny hat, they rock the Whitehall Theatre. It says so outside.

The characters they play? (Oh, peace, Miss Littlewood.) They are of indeterminate class. Upper-lower might be the best definition. There are hen-pecked husbands, formidable landladies, nice common girls, some in bathing suits, cretinous, adenoidal maids, irate fathers, all comic, all a downright disgrace to their class. And the busloads which should have rolled up to the Theatre Royal, Stratford East, roll up to the Whitehall instead.

I am just as confused by all this as anybody else. The difference is, I take it rather less seriously than some. For the popular theatre loves to create such anomalies.

It loves to create mysteries, too. Nobody knows how the road-shows of England originate, how they exist without support, and where they end. What immaculate conception creates those one-night performances in Bordeaux and Lyons? And how does *The Mousetrap* keep running? This play, we are told, is in its Tenth Imperishable year. Who on earth goes to see it now? Is there some kind of permanent audience, utterly dedicated, which sees it time and time again? Has the management come to 'an arrangement'? There have been dark hints recently that the play closed after one night, but that some paranoiac has created the myth of this monstrous run. This might bear investigation, because it is very difficult to find anybody who has actually seen the play.

This is all good stuff, though, well in line with the tradition and philosophy of show business. How it warms the heart to pass a theatre where a musical has opened the night before and see the notice 'Booking now for 1984'.

Such traditions must be respected. There have been too many inroads made into the popular theatre in the last few years. We have seen the musical in danger of becoming a social document. People have started adapting Dickens and Shaw. We must protect the amorous prawns of our theatre. Miss Evelyn Laye and Miss Cicely Courtneidge must never be allowed to appear in a play by Mr Arnold Wesker. The problems of *Probation Officer* must be kept to the little dark screen.

'The Countess Rosalie, deeply in love with Stefan, although secretly engaged to the repulsive Baron von Klopstenheim, retires to her castle. Her devoted friend, Blonda, madly in love with the Gypsy, Zstzy, although secretly engaged to the highly laughable Sosi Pfitzner, welcomes her. The gypsy band is heard...'

Oh, yes, it is the thing. Quite definitely the thing.

THE CHERRY ORCHARD

(1962)

The Cherry Orchard is sometimes seen in productions in this country as a work of brooding introspection: an examination of self in relation to the past. It is strange, therefore, to find Anton Chekhov writing to A P Chekhov in 1889 in the following way:

'The large large number of revisions need not trouble you, for the more of a mosaic the work is, the better. The characters stand to gain by this. The play will be worthless if all the characters resemble you.... Is there no life outside of you? And who is interested in knowing my life or yours, my thoughts and your thoughts? Give people people, and not yourself.'

It is unlikely that between the age of twenty-nine and forty-three Chekhov radically changed his view of work. The reference to a mosaic can apply to *The Cherry Orchard*. Should not the rest of the above quotation? But the fact is that we go to the play expecting to be moved emotionally. We expect to laugh. When neither happens we are disappointed. Something, we feel, has gone wrong in the staging of the play. But has it?

Should we not observe, certainly in a sympathetic way, but remain disengaged?

Is it not probable that Chekhov's plays are intended to produce an awareness of alienation, in the Brechtian sense of the word? Does not Chekhov's genius lie in the fact that he represents, more than that, creates *people* without the need to clothe them in the clammy emotionalism of lesser writers? Isn't this the reality of his characters? We laugh less and cry less outside the theatre than we would like to believe. We still, in spite of Brecht, like to cram into a couple of hours theatregoing our immediate emotional needs. Does Chekhov cheat us of this? Was it not, perhaps, his intention to do so?

Probably the answer to all these questions is no.

Yet there are misunderstandings about this play. There has long been the mystery of the sub-title. Chekhov himself described it as being 'not a drama but a comedy; in places almost a farce'. But if we say, as the dictionary does, that comedy is 'a branch of drama concerned with ordinary persons and employing familiar language', and that farce is 'an absurdly futile proceeding, a pretence, a mockery', we almost exactly describe *The Cherry Orchard.*

It is a play about revolution. A quiet revolution, certainly, but one as inexorable as a tide, and with forbidding undercurrents which Chekhov never lived to see realised. But his awareness is in every line of the play. Not far below the surface of these charming, lost people is a horrible, unresolved violence. Sometimes one or another of them is forced out into this unexplored and frightening land. Then they grasp at normality as they understand it. Gaev's incantation from the billiard table, for example, and Epihodov's delighted acceptance of his misfortunes. After all, these misfortunes are small compared with what lurks beneath the surface, round the corner, or a few days hence, and so can be positively enjoyed.

Jean-Louis Barrault has written of the end of the play in this way: 'This house, which two hours before was like a pregnant woman about to give birth, is now an icy tomb from which life has fled.' It might be more proper to say that the woman was aborted, for we are meant to be hurt, if not entirely horrified, by this play. In the last moments we see death, and nothing else.

I have heard people express disappointment with M. Michel Saint-Denis's production of *The Cherry Orchard,* which is now at the Aldwych Theatre. The grounds are not unusual, and are based on the misconceptions laid out above. This is certainly not a production to be seen for its emotional spree. But in its stillness, its exactness, its perfect observance of that element of time which is so peculiar to the play, it is an extraordinary and worthwhile experience. The art of direction in a play by Chekhov lies in the direction of the actors, an art at which M. Saint-Denis has always excelled.

This does not consist of any nonsense about *Imposing a Style* on a group of players, as is sometimes supposed, and indeed advocated. The style is dictated by the playwright. It is the director's job to reveal it through the actors.

Let us see how it has been managed in this case. I was recently taken to task for not describing in this theatre column actors' acting, as the late James Agate used to do. Let me use this opportunity to remedy the omission.

Madame Ranevsky is a silly woman. Charming, generous, amoral, weak, passionate and silly. It is hard to see her in the setting of today. Women seem to have become, most unfortunately, sensibly silly and spend their time now doing sensibly silly jobs. They no longer have difficulties, as Madame Ranevsky did, they have problems. For centuries men have attempted, but happily failed, to engage women in conversation. But now, with the long-range and deadly weapons of the newspaper, the radio and television, men have managed to explain women to women and, alas, the women have begun to understand themselves. And what is most unpleasant of all, they have begun to concern themselves with others than themselves.

None of these present-day considerations apply to Ranevsky. But they do to Dame Peggy Ashcroft's performance of the part. She is a little too much of our time. She is rather too aware, her horizons too wide. As Mr Kenneth Tynan has rightly pointed out, Ranevsky and Gaev are not aristocrats. But Ranevsky rules a tiny empire, which we see in decline, and if not an aristocrat, she is an autocrat. She obviously understands Lopahin's practical proposals for the future of the estate, but wilfully ignores them. Dame Peggy listens too well for a play by Chekhov. There are fine things here, though. There are the scenes with the daughters, and there is perfection in the reminiscence of the Paris episode. The passionate heart of Ranevsky beats in this, but it is only in retrospect.

Sir John Gielgud plays Gaev. It is a performance of such precision that it takes your breath away. See it again and again, search it, analyse it, and I defy anyone to fault it. It is impudent to write about such acting as this. It must be seen to be believed. The late James Agate at full stretch could not have done justice to it.

The scene – it cannot be more than twenty seconds long – where Gaev comes back after the sale of the cherry orchard, his little parcels of anchovies and her rings on his finger, tears in his eyes, petulance in his voice, is 'the best thing in the London theatre' at the moment.

Lopahin must suffer. Impelled by motives beyond his control, that is, a whole social movement, he must be aware that he tramples on delicate things, such as the hearts of Ranevsky and Gaev. There must be an element of remorse in his blindness. He is a man who needs love in spite of what he does.

Mr George Murcell, who plays Lopahin, performs the destruction well, but never once catches his breath at what he is doing. This man should be an enemy, certainly, but an enemy in spite of himself. It is his knowledge of self-inadequacy which stops him from proposing to Varya. Mr Murcell makes it a kind of foolish shyness, which is touching but not right.

The two daughters, Varya and Anya, are played by Miss Dorothy Tutin and Miss Judi Dench. Miss Tutin rightly never lets us forget that Varya is an adopted daughter. The fact is not insisted on in the play, but Miss Tutin keeps it before us throughout. She exists on sufferance. In her black dress with her housekeeper's keys, poised at the critical unmarried age of twenty-four, she is orphaned for life.

Miss Judi Dench is one of the few young actresses in England who can give us youth without girlishness, innocence without coyness. Her Anya in this production is certainly the best thing she has done so far. Watch her entrance in the third act with Trofimov to find her mother in tears. She approaches, is appalled, returns to the man for strength, gathers it, comes to her mother. All wordless, and yet in the moment is a world of growing up.

Trofimov is probably the most complex character in the play. Young enough to be in love with Anya and yet old enough to have been tutor to Ranevsky's dead son, invested with the classlessness of a poet, he spans both time and place. He is the one figure to break from his immediate surroundings.

Mr Ian Holm is excellent in this part. Deprecating, but accepting the jokes which are made about his appearance, his thought and his way of life, passionate but detached, this is probably the most truly Chekhovian performance in the play. It is satisfying to see an actor who obviously knows exactly what he is doing. An actor with a head as well as that vastly overestimated thing in the theatre, a heart. Mr Holm contains within the part that extraordinary sureness of purpose of the convinced revolutionary. There is something very disturbing in this uncanny prophetic voice which speaks of 1917.

Mr Roy Dotrice plays the unplayable Firs. How strange it is that great age is very often funny in the theatre, and never so in life. The fault must lie with Chekhov. Here is an example of a dramatist reaching too far out for the creation of a symbolic character. Mr Dotrice's performance seems to me one of great tact, although I believe he was accused in the early showing of the production of very much lacking this quality.

Miss Patience Collier repeats her performance as Charlotta, the governess. This wild doll of a woman, whose arbitrary behaviour disturbs the surface of the play, is a key figure. It is doubtful if it could be better done than it is done here.

Mr Paul Hardwick, as Pishchik brooding about Nietzsche, Mr Patrick Wymark as Epihodov nailing a box together, create their own worlds within this world. Mr David Buck as Yasha and Miss Patsy Byrne as Dunyasha show us the horror of people aping a life they are unfitted for, and do not care for.

There, this month I have surely done the actors proud. At least in the matter of space, if not in the matter of praise. It is not always so simple. Give an actor an inch, and he will take a column, and probably want a photograph too.

The production is the work of a master of the theatre. Has it inadequacies? Perhaps. Does the overall conception fail? Again perhaps. But anyway we should go down on our knees, or at least rush for seats, to see a production by Saint-Denis in England again. Am I talking like a sentimental man of the theatre, and not a critic? Well, I like to think of myself as the former.

It is a position needing more humility than the latter.

BRECHT IN ENGLISH

(1962)

The production of Bertolt Brecht's *The Caucasian Chalk Circle,* by the Royal Shakespeare Company at the Aldwych Theatre, is a theatrical event of great importance. It is the first major production of a play by Brecht to be done in this country in English. And it succeeds.

The play was written in America between 1943 and 1945. The translation at the Aldwych is by John Holmstrom, with four of the twelve songs translated by W H Auden. New music has been written for this production by Dudley Moore.

The story of the play is taken from Klabund's German adaptation of an old Chinese play, *The Circle of Chalk,* by way of an early short story by Brecht himself, *Der Augsburger Kreidekreis.*

The play begins in a village in the Caucasus at the end of the last war. Delegates from two collectives have met with an arbitrator over a land dispute. Members of the collectives then play out the story of The Chalk Circle, as an illustration of the philosophy of ownership. The story of the play is simple; the technical means chosen by Brecht to tell the story are complex and fascinating. This is one of the five great later plays, and it shows the man working at full imaginative stretch as an artist of the theatre. We see a superb arrogance of method, together with an elegant and almost mathematical form of structure.

After the first scene, which is a form of prologue, come three scenes which trace the journey of Grusche Vachnadze, the kitchen maid, with the governor's child, Michael. The second part of the play, in two scenes, tells the story of Azdak, the judge. This second part covers the same period of time as the first, and skilfully brings the protagonists together for the end, which is the decision on the ownership of the child by the true mother, or the foster-mother, Grusche. The scenes are linked, and sometimes commented on, by a narrator. Although strict, the form of the play allows for a lyrical gaiety which must be peculiar to this work.

The dialectic of the play has some strange conclusions, considering its origin. The children belong to those who are motherly; the land to those who will water it and make it fruitful. In short, it is a play about human love. And, curious for our time, love not confused by sex. The implications contained in the play about the law of possession are also very disturbing. It may be, and we can only hope it will be, fully understood in about 500 years time.

It was this play, on its production at the Theater am Schiffbauerdamm in June 1954, which reduced the party paper, *Neues Deutschland,* to complete silence. This takes some doing, and alone would give the work distinction. But in its playful way *The Caucasian Chalk Circle* is a minefield. *Sovietskaya Kultura,* reviewing the play on the occasion of the Berliner Ensemble's visit to Moscow in 1957, picked its way carefully through the detonators. The safe line to take was, as it always is, an accusation of formalism, and this the paper did. The negative characters of the play are masked. This is a fine uncontroversial point to be argumentative about, and the Soviet critic fastened on it with relief. It is like criticising *Hamlet,* and taking for your point of departure the advisability of using a skull as an object of meditation. It can be done, but it shows evasion to do it. To anyone interested in the details of this incident, and in the picture of an artist working in close, if uneasy, sympathy with a political creed, the facts can be found in Mr Martin Esslin's invaluable book, *Brecht: a Choice of Evils,* to which I am indebted.

The question which was asked when this Aldwych production of *The Caucasian Chalk Circle* was announced was can the play be done in English by English actors? The production completely vindicates the hope that it was possible.

First of all, there is the translation. This version by Mr Holmstrom would seem to be the first satisfactory *acting* version we have had of any of Brecht's plays. We must be grateful for the pioneer work of Eric Bentley and others which for many years made the plays available to the English reader, but when staged, these versions have never seemed successful.

Mr Holmstrom's translation is quick in humour, and the colloquialisms never made us uneasy. He has preserved the sour edge of Brecht's prose, and only once or twice do the lines go soft, and these mainly in the part of Grusche. The overall impression of the translation in performance is that it is strong and faithful to the original. The English theatre has lacked good working versions of German plays for many years. This is probably the reason for the German repertory being less well-known in this country than, say, the French. The plays of Hauptmann, for example, and it is only one example of many, stay virtually unknown in our theatre. There are a great many plays that Mr Holmstrom could turn his attention and talent towards. We must hope he does so.

The production is by Mr William Gaskill. He has very faithfully followed Brecht's text, with no startling or unnerving shortening of it in any place. The staging of the play is in mood, and much of its method, close to the production by the Berliner Ensemble. The setting of the play by Mr Ralph Koltai closely follows the setting by von Appen. Yet this is in no way a reproduction. Simply, Mr Gaskill has not been muddled by Brecht's own production, and tried to be violently different: I suppose the proper word today is 'original'. And by not being intimidated, Mr Gaskill retained the play's vitality and form. It is a fine achievement.

There may have been fears before this production about the capability of English actors to perform the plays of Brecht. Earlier productions did not produce happy results. Not only are the plays of a formal structure in both language and dramatic shape, but they have long existed in the heavy shadow of Brecht's theory of acting. Both form and theory are alien to much of the best kind of English acting. The general standard of acting in this country is higher now than ever before. It is a debatable point as to whether it is the best in the world, but it would certainly have a claim. Yet in spite of its excellence, it has been narrow in range. This has been both its strength and its weakness. Its strength because the very narrowness has given it a concentrated power in English classical plays and naturalistic drama; its weakness because it has not allowed outside influence to enlarge or encourage its growth, and so given the art the capability to perform foreign classics in translation without turning them into pastiche. The unifying style imposed by Mr Gaskill upon his company at the Aldwych should silence the critics who complain that English actors generally, and the members of this theatre company in particular, are unable to perform in ensemble style.

Miss Patsy Byrne plays Grusche. She is gentler and more placid than Angelica Hurwicz in the part. (Some comparison is unavoidable.) Hurwicz was touched by tragedy. Miss Byrne inclines to pathos. She gives everything to the child, both love and care, but Hurwicz extended the part in an extraordinary way by drawing *from* the child both hope and endurance. This was an extension which raised the part to a high point of tragedy. This said, there is nothing but praise for Miss Byrne. Her love scenes with the soldier, Simon, are beautifully done. And they are not easy to do. Brecht always had difficulty in coming to grips with the representation of human love at its most ordinary level. He was forced to resort to strange devices such as the reporting of speech between the lovers by a narrator, as in this play. It is not that Brecht knew too little about the sexual situation, it is that he knew too much, and so kept its representation under strict control.

Azdak, the judge, is played by Mr Hugh Griffith. This performance, I think, must be considered wholly successful. Mr Griffith is that most exciting kind of actor whose eccentricity does not exist in a vacuum, but is put to the cause of reality. He is a daring actor, shocking the purists, and then delighting everyone by demonstrating that nothing he does is in the end arbitrary, but a mosaic of meaning. He flares, and so is the perfect actor for Azdak. And this is a rare character, equal in range to many of Shakespeare's finest.

Coming away from a performance of this play, we must be reminded that Brecht was working in the later plays towards a new form of playwriting, which was never completely achieved. Had he been given another ten or fifteen

NOTES

John Whiting gave his lecture 'The Art of the Dramatist' at the Old Vic on 29 September 1957, and an excerpt was printed in the November 1957 issue of *Plays and Players*. The whole text appears in *The Art of the Dramatist*. (See Bibliography.)

'Writer as Gangster', the interview with Clive Goodwin and Tom Milne, editors of *Encore*, was published in *Encore* No.29, Vol.8, No.1, January–February 1961, and the interview with Richard Findlater in *Time and Tide*, 9 March 1961.

'Writing for Actors' appeared in *The Adelphi*, second quarter 1952, and 'A Conversation' in *Nimbus*, June-August 1953. 'Half Time at the Royal Court' was published in *Truth*, 8 November 1957, and 'At Ease in a Bright Red Tie' in *Encore*, September-October 1959. 'A New English Theatre' was a contribution to a symposium in *The London Magazine*, July 1960.

The first instalment of 'From My Diary' was published in *Twentieth Century*, February 1961.

'Inside the Asylum', 'One and One Make One', 'A Good Laugh', '*The Kitchen*', '*Luther*', 'Some Notes on Acting', 'The Popular Theatre', '*The Cherry Orchard*' and 'Brecht in English' appeared in the monthly *The London Magazine* between April 1961 and August 1962, when Whiting was its drama critic.

He also wrote for *The Times*, the *Observer*, the *New Statesman*, the *Spectator* and *Vogue*. The other pieces in this book appeared previously in *The Art of the Dramatist*.

BIBLIOGRAPHY

The Plays of John Whiting (London, 1957.)
> Contains *Saint's Day, A Penny for a Song* and *Marching Song.*

The Devils (London, 1961.)

No Why (London, 1961.)

Collected Plays, 2 vols ed. Ronald Hayman. (London, 1969.)
> Vol 1 contains *Conditions of Agreement, Saint's Day, A Penny for a Song* and *Marching Song.* Vol 2 contains *The Gates of Summer, No Why, A Walk in the Desert, The Devils, Noman* and *The Nomads.*

No More A-Roving (London, 1975.)

The Art of the Dramatist, ed. Ronald Hayman (London, 1969.)
> Contains the lecture which had that title, some fragments of fiction and a selection of critiques.

John Whiting on Theatre (London, 1966.)
> Contains 13 pieces, mostly reviews of plays, written for the *London Magazine,* between April 1961 and August 1962.

Translations

Jean Anouilh *Traveller without Luggage* (London, 1959.)

Jean Anouilh *Madame de...* (London, 1959.)

André Obey *Sacrifice to the Wind* in *Three Dramatic Legends* ed. Elizabeth Haddon, (London, 1964.)

Books on Whiting

Ronald Hayman *John Whiting* (London, 1969.)

Simon Trussler *The Plays of John Whiting: An Assessment* (London, 1972.)

Eric Salmon *The Dark Journey: John Whiting as Dramatist* (London, 1979.)

In its appendices, this book contains variant endings of *The Gates of Summer,* a 1950 letter from Whiting to Peter Brook about the production of *A Penny for a Song* Brook was about to direct at the Haymarket, and cast lists for the first productions of Whiting's major plays.